CONCHITA'S SPIRITUAL JOURNEY

CONCHITA'S SPIRITUAL JOURNEY

THE GREAT STAGES

IGNACIO NAVARRO ALFARO, M.SP.S.

ST PAULS

Library of Congress Cataloging-in-Publication Data
Navarro, Ignacio, 1918-1980.
  [Itinerario espiritual de Concepción Cabrera de Armida. English]
  Conchita's spiritual journey : the great stages / Ignacio Navarro.
    p. cm.
  Translation of: Itinerario espiritual de Concepción Cabrera de Armida.
  "Translated from the second Spanish edition of 1982"—T.p. verso.
  ISBN-13: 978-0-8189-1320-4
  ISBN-10: 0-8189-1320-7
  1. Conchita, 1862-1937.   I. Title.
  BX4705.C742N28 2010
  282.'092—dc22
  [B]   2010008761

Produced and designed in the United States of America by the
Fathers and Brothers of the Society of St. Paul,
2187 Victory Boulevard, Staten Island, New York 10314-6603
as part of their communications apostolate.

ISBN-10: 0-8189-1320-7
ISBN-13: 978-0-8189-1320-4

Printing Information:

Current Printing - first digit	1	2	3	4	5	6	7	8	9	10

Year of Current Printing - first year shown

2010	2011	2012	2013	2014	2015	2016	2017	2018	2019

TABLE OF CONTENTS

FOREWORD

Dear reader, the title of this book is pretentious. I openly confess it to you. The spiritual journey of this great woman would necessitate an ample and significant number of volumes and a much more significant writer. This is at best a superficial description of the most important moments along her spiritual pathway.

Don't expect too much. Nor should you expect too little, in light of God's word to His handmaid: *"Through the presence of the Word in your soul, I have, in a certain sense, made you a word."* Conchita is the word that the Lord speaks to us.

In these pages, she is the one who does the communicating. My work has been simply to choose a few hundred texts from the thousands in her diary, from her life and other writings, and to piece them together. Perhaps there might be others that are better, but these seemed timely to me.

I trust in the effectiveness of the words of this Servant of God. (In 1999, His Holiness Pope John Paul II declared María de la Concepción Cabrera de Armida "Venerable Servant of God.")

Let us praise God, Who is admirable in His saints; let us thank the Lord for the marvelous graces that He deigned to pour forth on a mother with such an ordinary family life; let us ask that we may be able to follow in her footsteps of love and sacrifice with Christ for the glory of God and the salvation of humankind.

Ignacio Navarro Alfaro
Missionary of the Holy Spirit

ACKNOWLEDGMENTS

These pages contain the text from conferences
which were dictated by the author
on various occasions.
Translated from the second Spanish edition of 1982
Final editing by James Wierzbicki
Editing team: Ron Leonardo
Mary McCandless
Dolores Icaza RCSCJ
Cecilia Corona RCSCJ
Irma C. Peniche, RCSCJ

INTRODUCTION

We intend to present in these pages the spiritual journey of a woman: Concepción Cabrera de Armida — a secular woman, spouse and mother. She is from our century. Four of her children are still living [as of 1980]. She died on March 3, 1937.

Perhaps many will ask, "What meaning does presenting the spiritual journey of a mystic have today?" My response is that *Conchita's Spiritual Journey* has to do with a mystic in the most noble and authentic expression of the word.

Does it not seem to deal with a topic outside reality as we know it? Christian movements of our day and age — in thought and activity — are more attentive to the "horizontal" dimension that is, to people's relationships with one another, the community and the world — rather than to the vertical dimension, which concerns their relationship with God. The vertical dimension was emphasized in its day. Now it seems to belong to the past.

In our day, it is thought necessary to encounter God in man, in our brothers and sisters: i.e., in the social dimensions of life. The mystic is outside the times. The Church itself, through the renewing impetus of the Second Vatican Council, propels us toward a dialogue with the world, with everyone. The signs of the times indicate a pathway toward man.

This manner of thinking holds a great deal of truth in it that is positive, but it would be incomplete, and even false, if this approach were exclusive.

The horizontal approach, in order to be realized, needs the vertical. The horizontal crosspiece of the cross is not sustained in midair, but has to be supported by the vertical piece, firmly rooted in the ground and then raised toward heaven. Concern for others, for their sake, is legitimate, but it has its limits. Only "a greater love" is able to surpass those limits. *"There is no greater love than to lay down one's life for one's friend,"* Jesus told us (Jn 15:13). In fact, that "greater love" — that which is able to achieve continued heroism — has its font in God, Who is Love. Those who distance themselves from that font end up thirsty. In the desert of injustice and sin, thirst can signify death... the death of love.

The vertical dimension — the encounter with the living God — is as indispensable now as it ever was. In fact, it is needed more today than ever.

The experience of God, common to the mystic who is transformed into a witness of His presence and of His divine action in the world, is very important and necessary in our century, which has gone so far as to speak of the death of God. The encounter with God continues to be the inspiration and font behind the encounter with man, even to the point of heroism.

We encounter both God and man in Jesus. Nobody lived the horizontal dimension as He did — in all its breadth and depth. He is the Savior of all. He came *"so that we might have life and have it to the full"* (Jn 10:10). He loved us *"to the end"* (Jn 13:1) and He offered Himself on the cross for us all. His entire life was for others. "For us men and for our salvation He came down from heaven and became flesh of the Virgin Mary" (cf. the Nicene Creed).

Nor has anyone lived the vertical dimension more intensely and profoundly than He as man. Recourse to His Father was constant. He passed entire nights praying to God. *"My food is to do the will of My Father"* (cf. Jn 4:34). *"I always do what is pleasing to My Father"* (cf. Jn 8:29). The mission of Christ as Savior embraces the fullness of both dimensions, the horizontal and the vertical, and unifies them. The purpose of His becoming incarnate in human flesh is the glory of God in the salvation of humankind.

The Church is the mysterious extension of Christ throughout the centuries. It makes the presence of God, the Savior of men, real and perceptible in the midst of men: those of yesterday, those of today and those of tomorrow. Its mission is to continue that of Christ, which is the glory of God in the salvation of men: *"By this is My Father glorified: that you bear much fruit and become My disciples"* (Jn 15:18).

Two great affirmations contained in the most important Conciliar Constitutions form the important nucleus of the renewal of the Church that came out of the Second Vatican Council: first, in the Pastoral Constitution, *Gaudium et Spes*, we are told that there is but one vocation of humankind: the divine vocation. In that single vocation there is an offering and a call to the integral salvation of humankind body and soul — in time and for eternity. Second, in the Constitution on the Church, *Lumen Gentium*, we are given the universal call to holiness.

Such a profound renewal lies not only in the reform of this or that structure, or in the vision of the People of God and the hierarchy, or in the co-responsibility of all in the People of God, but in the fact that this co-responsibility — through the call of God — has to be brought to completion. This fullness of life and of love is called sanctity. Each and every member of the People of God is called to sanctity. This is not an extraordinary or rare goal, or an inheritance for just a few. It is an invitation that our Lord makes to all.

A great Jewish philosopher of our century — Henri Bergson — stated that the mystic is humankind realized in its fullness — a human being fully realized. It is "superman," but without pride. He was right. The mystic, by definition, is one who has experienced God. Humankind, open to what is transcendent of its very nature, can only be fully realized in its fullness through the encounter with the living and transcendent God.

To underscore the various stages on the journey, through which the Lord leads a person meekly responding to the divine call toward the deepest experience of God, is not old-fashioned. Even less so is the presentation of a laywoman who lived and died in the twentieth century. Family life was the hallmark of her existence. Her mission was totally for the sake of others — in other words, the horizontal dimension — but it had as its source the intimate and profound experience of God, the vertical dimension.

Presenting *Conchita's Spiritual Journey* is not the unearthing of useless memories from the past, nor is it a triumphalism without meaning. It is placing before the eyes of the world today a witness of God. It is to throw light on a concrete goal fulfilled to which God is inviting everyone. It is to point out a figure of the present times whom the Lord wanted to mold as a herald of the future.

Could there be anything more timely? I am convinced that God wants it and that we need it.

It is not my intention, in these pages, to present the biography of the Servant of God, Concepción Cabrera de Armida. I intend only to indicate the great stages of her spiritual journey. It is not possible to totally do away with days and dates, because these are historical facts; I indicate them only as points of reference.

Like a painter, the Divine Artist arranges the canvas (the first step), lays out the basic colors and outlines the figure in the background (the second step). Then, with divine strokes, He accomplishes His master work (the third step) and turns it over to His Church (the fourth step).

These great stages practically coincide with the important dates in the life of Conchita:

1862-1884 – From birth to marriage (preparation)

1885-1902 – Married life until the death of her husband: The solid base of her spiritual life.

1903-1917 – The Central Grace: preparation and immediate consequences.

1917-1937 – Her influence upon the Church: Her spiritual maternity grows.

THE FIRST STAGE
(1862 - 1884)

PREPARATION

The extraordinary gifts of God are abundant in the following stages in Conchita's life. The Lord takes her to the pinnacle of union with Him. Upon looking at the whole of God's work in her, it is a strong temptation to interpret all the events of her life, even those that in any other person appear normal or simple coincidences, in light of His later graces.

There would remain the impression that she belongs to a special breed, someone exceptional from infancy. Many would say, thus a saint was born. This is not the reality. Conchita's childhood and youth seemed much the same as that of many other girls and young ladies of her time and place, without denying the intervention of Providence and the love of God. She herself commented about her childhood: "I got angry with my siblings. I fought with them, disobeyed my parents, stole candy or fruit, and told lies — horrible, at times! I later made up for it, and then once again offended my Jesus." She was a child the same as many others. Anecdotes about her childhood and youth are plentiful, as they are in all families.

By contrast the deeds and characteristics relating to her spiritual journey are few: as a little girl, she experienced a dream and an event, that of her first communion; in her youth, she attended her first dance, met her only boyfriend, and suffered the tragic event of the death of her older brother.

A dream

"From the time I was a little girl" (around six years old), "I had a dream... or I don't know what it was, but it has remained recorded in my memory, and even more, in my heart.

"I saw the living Lord, full of life, dressed in a purple vestment made of velvet, resting on my skirts; that is to say that His head was on me, I being seated on the ground. I was playing with His silken curls, with His hair, with great love and respect; and He, every once in a while, would look at me, turning His azure eyes upward and, in that look, bathed me with a divine sensation that I had never felt before. This lasted a good while, and even after so many years I have not been able to forget it. I remember that it moved me deeply."

Even though it may have been only a dream, it was the grace of God. The indelible impression that this Divine Glance of immense tenderness left on her would become a magnet that attracted her to our Lord from that moment on.

First Holy Communion

She made her first Holy Communion on her tenth birthday. There was nothing out of the ordinary: "Because of my own lukewarm attitude and laziness, I don't remember anything particular about that day, except an immense internal pleasure and joy over my white dress." It was undoubtedly important in her spiritual journey, because then began her love of the Eucharist, which constantly grew and would become one of her characteristics: "From that time on, my love for the Eucharist continued to grow, and I had particular joy in frequenting the sacraments until, when I was fifteen or sixteen years old, they let me receive Communion even four or five times a week, and a little while later, daily."

In her personal diary, there are repeated expressions that manifest to us the consequences of this event: "my adored Eucharist"; "the Eucharist that is my delight"; "an indispensable necessity for my life." It is very important to note the intervention of Divine Providence here since, before the decree of Saint Pius X regarding the Eucharist, it was very rare to permit the reception of Holy Communion so frequently.

First dance

Shortly after her fourteenth birthday, she attended her first dance and continued attending dances over the course of many years. One day she heard the voice of the Lord telling her, *"I want you to go to the dance."* In the middle of the dance, she discovered the riches of the cross and resolved to embrace it. Her social life — dances, visits, the theater and social gatherings — formed a part of the pathway that God had chosen for her.

A single boyfriend

At that first dance, she met her only boyfriend and her future spouse. A month later, they had both fallen in love and that love several years later took her to marriage and motherhood, which would be simultaneously the defining characteristic of her life and the veil that hid the extraordinary graces of God, even while providing the opportunity to practice heroic virtues naturally and with great simplicity.

Eight years of a pure and simple courtship went by. "Our courtship never worried me in the sense that it would cause me to belong less to God. It was so easy for me to bring both things together! When I went to bed and even when I was alone, I thought of Pancho and later of the Eucharist, which was my delight. Every day I went to Communion and later would see him pass by: the memory of Pancho did not hinder my prayers. I would adorn myself and get dressed up just to please him; I went to the theater and to the dances just to see him; nothing else mattered to me. Yet in the midst of all of this, I did not forget my God. Most of the time, I remembered Him and He attracted me in an indescribable manner."

A mournful event

Conchita was about nineteen years old when her older brother Manuel was entertaining a visitor and having coffee. When he sat down, the trigger of his pistol caught and fired. The bullet penetrated Manuel's head and he died instantly. "This blow was very cruel, but very healthful not only for my poor soul, which was so torn and distracted, but also for my entire family. During the period of mourning, I went back to giving myself more to God, to thinking more about Him, separating myself from the current that was taking me toward the vanities of this earth."

Dancing, going steady, mourning. These take place in the lives of many young people. Anecdotes could be numerous. The characteristic traits are encompassed in a few phrases: A girl like so many others, with qualities and defects. A simple and candid young person — she called herself foolish — like so many others of her time and of her city.

Preparation

The Lord was preparing her with His grace — the same grace that He offers to everyone — and which is manifested:

1) In a tender and purified love of the Eucharist,
2) In a desire to please Jesus even at the cost of sacrifice and giving things up,
3) In the complete integration of her love of her betrothed with the love of God,
4) In the attraction toward solitude and silence, the expression of her longing and nostalgia for God.

"Ever since I was a little girl, the countryside, the birds, nature, its peace and its sunrises and sunsets always transported my soul to God. The solitude of the forests delighted me, and I found myself always singing in the forest; sometimes the ecstasies of my soul toward the Creator of everything were so strong that I would make certain that I stayed behind to enjoy in silence all that which absorbed me. Later, I enjoyed visiting the poor and even envied them."

Graces of God? Certainly, but of the type that God does not deny to anyone who asks them of Him and wishes to live as a Christian. They are in the reach of all, whatever their condition or state of life.

Without a doubt, beginning with this stage of Conchita's journey, there was an intervention from Divine Providence that we indeed could call extraordinary in two very characteristic aspects: the preservation of the innocence and purity of her soul and the light to see that the love of Jesus is expressed in voluntary sacrifice. That divine preservation and her love of the cross were preparation for later graces. Later on, the Lord would make her see very clearly and repeatedly how both things were indispensable for the realization of His divine plan for her.

Why did Conchita marry?

Let's place ourselves into the mentality of that time. The common feeling — among priests and laypeople — was that favored souls had a place in the religious life and the priesthood. The state of marriage was good for mediocre souls, those of the second class, who did not aspire to sainthood. A woman with higher visions, who would feel strongly the attraction of divine love, would have no other place to go than into the cloistered convent, into a life consecrated to the Lord.

Conchita carried in her soul — by the grace of God — that tremendous desire to love the Lord. Exquisitely refined, innocent, pure, and also totally ignorant of the intimacy of marriage, she would undoubtedly have opted for the road of the cloister.

But the Lord had His own plans for her, hidden plans that would be revealed little by little over time. Meanwhile, He placed a blindfold over her eyes. As a child, she only knew sisters in the active religious life and she thought that to consecrate oneself to God in a life of the cloister belonged to ancient times and no longer existed.

Years later, one of her confessors, Father Espinoza de los Monteros, upon realizing the ardor and the devotion of her love for Jesus, as well as the sensitivity of her soul, proposed the religious life to her. He had not realized that she was married and already had four children. "It was the only thing he did not guess about me," Conchita commented.

She was unaware of her path as a pioneer. She did not know that the Lord had given her a mission as a prophetic sign for our times: the sanctity and fruitfulness of a married laywoman in the Church.

During the years of her courtship, she knew only that she wanted to love our Lord very much, and in her visits to the tabernacle, she repeated to Him many times: "Lord, I do not know how to love You. I want to marry so that You can give me many children who will love You better than I." How would she have known that she would have thousands of spiritual children that would extend her love? She also believed that upon marrying she would have greater freedom for prayer and penance.

The Lord wanted to establish a solid basis for her spiritual life and sanctity, enriching her with abundant graces of union with Him, and initiating Conchita's admirable fruitfulness in the Church during her married life.

But she was not aware of that. Only years later did the Lord begin to draw back the veil from His plans of love. *"I have My goals which you do not know and I am able to communicate with souls in all states of life. The world will receive an example of My power and many souls will be sanctified through this means."* Then Conchita commented, "I understood that the Lord wanted — when I die or I don't know when — to make His goodness shine upon a poor married woman, or better said, that His great power would be seen in all states of life.... I do not even want to think about this and so I close my eyes and walk embracing the cross only through obedience."

THE SECOND STAGE
(1885 - 1902)

ON THE ROAD TOWARD UNION

The married life of the Servant of God spanned seventeen years less seven weeks: from November 8, 1884 until September 17, 1901, the day on which her husband died. They are the years in which the Lord took her by the hand with divine pedagogy, forming her little by little. Those graces which we clearly see as the most noteworthy have their own fruitfulness and are a step that leads toward the step which follows.

In this chapter, we are able to distinguish four short stages, or periods, that spontaneously distinguish themselves one from another:

From her marriage to the first spiritual exercises (1884-1889);

Her search for a spiritual director (1889-1893);

The dizzying ascent toward union (1893-1897);

The pinnacle of her union with Christ and the beginning of her preparation for the central grace; Christ-like virtues; the death of her husband (1897-1902).

Newlywed

In her marriage, Conchita looked for human happiness — as is only natural. But deeper and beyond that human realization was her yearning for God. "Upon seeing, in spite of my husband's goodness," she wrote years later, "that marriage was not the kind of fulfillment that I had thought it would be, my heart instinctively went more and more toward God, seeking in Him all that was lacking, but my interior emptiness grew in spite of all earthly joys." Some would call this frustration or alienation. Saint Augustine, in his psychological astuteness, calls it something else: "You made us for Yourself, Lord, and our hearts wander restlessly until they rest in You." It is called a yearning for the infinite.

Firm and constant steps in her spiritual life began a short while later in her marriage, and thus in 1893, she was able to write, "During this period of my spiritual life as I can see with greater clarity from this vantage point nine years later, Jesus had much to lament regarding my inconstancy and limited generosity."

During those first years of marriage, her desire to give herself more and more to God continued to grow, but she did not know how to bring it about. She met the first nuns from a religious order — those of the Sacred Heart — who had founded a school in San Luis Potosí and she started to regularly frequent their chapel. "I felt a holy envy in my soul. I prayed with many tears in that chapel." She did not see another way of totally belonging to God except through the cloistered convent, and she was already married. "Several times I tried to unburden my heart with one of the sisters, but the ones that I spoke with almost never understood me. 'How does one love God?' I asked them, because this was my concern and my yearning: to know how to love Him deliriously. 'What is virtue?' I often asked myself, since my soul would demand of me at the top of its voice that I know them and practice them. I passed long periods of time with this thought, lamenting that I did not understand what I wanted to follow."

The sacramental grace of matrimony, in a soul well-disposed to look for God above all things, produced an ever-more ardent desire to belong to Him without leaving behind the obligations of her state in life.

In search of a director

In August of 1889, she was about to celebrate five years of marriage, and already had three children. She attended a retreat being preached by Fr. Plancarte "coming and going, because I could not leave my children." She had already heard some of the talks on other retreats directed by Monsignor Amézquita, but "the first exercises that I heard preached were those of Fr. Plancarte. I don't know how to describe what caught my attention and moved my soul.

"One day, on which I was preparing with all my soul for that which the Lord wanted of me, at the very moment that the priest stated these words which amazed me, I listened clearly in the depths of my soul, without being able to doubt it: '*Your mission is that of saving souls.*' I did not understand how I would be able to do this. It seemed so rare and so impossible. I thought that it would be in sacrificing myself in favor of my husband, children and servants."

This interior word that Conchita heard "without being able to doubt it," and that she did not even understand, indicates an important moment in her spiritual journey. It is like a barely enunciated melody, very soon to be transformed into the central theme of a marvelous symphony. The orchestra will fully execute it over and over again in many tones and with infinite variations.

In such a manner, she remained convinced of the worth of these spiritual exercises and of the abundant fruit that she had experienced within herself. From that time on, she practiced them each year until the end of her life. Much later, the Lord would tell her repeatedly, *"You were born for others... your life is for others... it does not belong to you."* Thus, God's plan began to be revealed in those first exercises.

Their immediate fruit was manifest in two ways, above all: a burning zeal on behalf of souls and a growing intimacy with Jesus. We see this in her own words:

"With this growing fire in my heart, zeal devoured me and I was anxious to share my joy and the sublime teachings that I had learned." At the hacienda she met with sixty women and transmitted what she had heard "and just as in the land of the blind the person with one eye is king, the poor very much liked what I was telling them and they cried and were moved to contrition.... I felt happy speaking about Jesus and His Most Holy Mother....

"One day, shortly after the spiritual exercises, I was walking in the garden of the hacienda Jesús María saying my prayers when I felt the most vivid desire to invite our Lord to accompany me. Everything made me feel as if He were clearly united with me, walking on the path that I was walking. Later, full of love and gratitude, I began to chat with Him and I heard His extremely sweet and gentle voice, which told me that I should always call on Him with a great deal of confidence; that I should invite Him in the morning so He might show me how to walk in His presence all day, and that I should listen to Him, chat with Him and take Him to all my activities. He told me that I should figure on having Him not only inside me, but also at my side, always watching me. That when I was sleeping, I would be resting on His Divine Heart. That the more I invited Him, the sooner I would see myself as needing His company. Until the day arrived in which we would not be separated for an instant. Afterward, He left and I remained with a void which could not be filled.

"The next day I called Him and thus it was for a long time. He always came… He always came this way, in the future, would help me to see Him and feel Him joined to me. Upon passing through a doorway, I would let Him go first; upon sitting down while I sewed I would place a chair next to me for Him…. When I went to the kitchen to make bread, to play the piano and even when breastfeeding the children, He was always with me."

Her zeal for the salvation of souls, which had been born in her heart, and her growing intimacy with Jesus led Conchita to look for a hand that would lead her with security through the pathways of the spirit: a spiritual director. She encountered various confessors of whom she asked help, but either they did not understand her or God did not enlighten them:

"I had come to a point, through the favor of God, at which my confessors told me that I had reached perfection, and nevertheless it did not satisfy me, because I had another, more lofty idea, undoubtedly infused by God, in the depth of my soul, and that degree of virtue seemed so meager to me and so lowly, that my heart cried a thousand times out of profound sadness and discouragement... as if there had been placed a great insurmountable obstacle before me, but I, without knowing why, was fighting in order to take it from my path, certain that something greater existed a little beyond that, something infinite to occupy my spiritual life....

"I felt more than ever the need for support, but where could I find it? I felt strange feelings in my soul, virtues as if in a cocoon, I might say, longing to open up. A hunger for the divine, a burning thirst for Jesus, but it was as if this hunger were blocking me, as if I were losing myself on a pathway of obscure faith without hope.

"Occasionally, when my soul was bursting to communicate, to speak about God, His goodness, His beauty, His attributes in general, a priest might come up with some poetry about nature, the heavens, the earth, the twilight; things, yes, that lead you to God, but they are not God Himself. The essence of poetry — its focus or ideal, I would say — was what I carried imprinted in the depths of my spirit.... That ideal was the focus of my hope and I was desperate in knowing neither how to pray nor having anyone who would teach me how, not even one who would speak to me about it...!

"Alone, with the clearest graces of the Holy Spirit, which really guided a large part of my life, I went along until I came to a point where I was halted, kept back, until God granted me (blessed may He be!) a soul who felt as I did, who would understand and guide me."

This second stage of her married life ends at Conchita's meeting her true spiritual director: Father Alberto Cuscó Mir,

S.J., a man with solid doctrine and great apostolic zeal. He was the instrument chosen by God to establish the bases of Conchita's spiritual life with a robust and firm background in the school of that great instructor in the ways of the spirit, Saint Ignatius of Loyola.

Toward Divine Union

Upon Father Mir's discovery of the high aspirations of his directee, the urgent call of God to sanctity, and the generosity of her answer, he dedicated himself to examining the deep foundations in her soul which would leave a profound mark on her spirituality. This follows the advice of Saint Augustine: "The higher you wish to raise the structure of sanctity, the more you have to think about the profound foundation of humility."

"Humility, humility," he repeated to her. "Clothe yourself in your nothingness; humble yourself, disregard yourself." He taught her that her prayer should always begin with a review of her poverty and her weaknesses. Later, the light of God would make her see more and more clearly the immensity and grandeur of the Lord and her own insignificance and smallness: the nothingness of her being. At the same time as it protected her against the temptation of selfishness, self-satisfaction and narcissism, the recognition of her nothingness attracted the graces of God upon her: *"I descend toward you, because you do not rise."*

From that time forward, sentiments regarding her insignificance, her spiritual modesty, and humility in the face of divine favors — her expressions are innumerable — are constant in Conchita, and many times she wishes to hide herself beneath the earth, as if overwhelmed by the divine graces.

Together with humility, the indispensable foundation of the spiritual life, her spiritual director moves her toward obedience, which prevents the danger of illuminism: i.e., a doctrine advocating enlightenment and subjective delusion in a life abounding with extraordinary graces. She docilely submits everything, including her communications with the Lord and His graces regarding prayer, to the approval of her director. Sacrifice, the touchstone that unmasks the sentimentality of love, is another of the basic elements of that spiritual direction.

Humility, obedience, sacrifice: the guarantees of a solid spiritual life. How invaluable a good spiritual director is.

Let us see, for example, some of the advice that he gave to her and that she carefully wrote and saved:

"'In order to reach perfection,' he told me, 'it is necessary that the Holy Spirit, the soul and the director reach a common agreement. Therefore, clarity of conscience, discretion, humility and obedience are indispensable.

"'Humility is the truth. Throw away your pride, throw away your pride! Humble yourself, humble yourself,' he repeated to me. 'God is everything, you are nothing.' He repeated this to me over and over again. 'There is no height without lowliness. Embrace your poverty. There is no road that leads to God other than humility and your own self-contempt.... The beginning, the middle, and the end of perfection is humility.

"'To humble yourself,' he told me, 'to crush yourself, to lose yourself in oblivion and in self-effacement, as if you were in a pigsty.' In this way, he imbued me with self-awareness. Humility is the weapon that has never failed when used as a fundamental point in my spiritual direction. He explained obedience in so many ways. He made me love it. Hearing this voice, the hardest thing became easy for me.

"How his direction united love and sacrifice in my soul! 'That is what is special in your spirit,' he repeated to me: 'I cannot oppose the plans that I discern that God has for you, even though you are inconsequential.

"'Onward toward sacrifice, onward toward sacrifice! This is a cry that issues from the depth of my soul when you approach me. Embrace the cross. Onward toward sacrifice, my daughter! Do not be afraid. Braced with humility, hidden and obedient, you cannot get lost. I watch over your soul. Continue your path.

"'Tears are flowing from my eyes upon writing this to you, but it seems clear to me that you are destined for the cross, with all of its consequences. Thus, you will save souls. For you, this is the only way that there is, but be sure that you will save many thousands. You will not know it while you are living, because your life is to be hidden without knowledge of the results until eternity.

"'Even when you do not understand the prayer let yourself be lifted up by it, since the Holy Spirit is the one who directs you and I will stand guard. Do not put up obstacles to grace. God wants you very high. You must give Him much glory, but on the cross and through the cross.' He said that I had to double the time lost, because he knew that the Lord was calling me, and that He had goals for this poor scrub brush."

That spiritual direction, in all of its aforementioned aspects, prepared Conchita for a torrent of extraordinary graces, with the guarantee of obedience and humility, and for the foundation — amidst thorns — of the Works of the Cross.

She herself summarizes her feelings:

"How he unfurled the sails of my soul, making it fly, enjoying its freedom, its inclinations, supporting the Lord's plans for it. What insights he had about the future and how to remove the obstacles and the stumbling blocks with integrity, with firmness and with charity."

In addition to these very concrete aspects, her spiritual director guided her toward other attitudes that united all of her acts: e.g., to avoid deliberate offenses, to always have right intentions and to do what is most perfect.

"'The right intention,' he told me, 'prevents falls, having a firm will to never offend God! Our gaze must be fixed on Christ for our encouragement, our self-knowledge always in sight. We must be aware of our own insignificance so that we do not fill ourselves with pride, and mindful of our weakness in order to humble ourselves.' He rapidly brought her to formally promise to avoid all deliberate offenses — a negative aspect of the spiritual life — while orienting her to a proper balance so as to avoid scruples and useless anxiety. Later, he invited her to do that which was best — also with a formal promise — with the understanding that, among various options, it was necessary to always choose that which she believed to be the most pleasing to God. In other words, to please God in everything.

Throughout her life, Conchita maintained an immense gratitude for this spiritual director and her spirituality remained deeply marked by the school of Ignatius. We, also, are very grateful to him: not only for the great good that he did for Conchita and for the firmness and decisiveness with which he helped her to advance with giant steps, but also for that direction and obedience that he knew how to instill in her and to which the most abundant and admirable pages of her personal diary are indebted. Even more, we are grateful for the fact that she did not destroy them.

Monogram

There is one event in Conchita's life that is of great importance in her spiritual journey and in her mission. It is an act that, if not placed in its actual context, is disconcerting to many and to some it is a cause for horror and rejection. It is the act of having engraved Jesus's monogram, JHS, on her chest.

What is the actual context? In her married life, and even more in her adolescence and youth, Conchita had spent many seasons in the haciendas and on ranchos. She loved to go horseback riding — in fact she went as far as Saltillo — and was familiar with everything referring to field animals: testing the mettle of young bulls, going to rodeos, shoeing horses and branding. She had been present many times when the initials of the owner were branded on the animals with a red hot iron.

On the other hand, there was her psychological makeup. In her writings, we often find the phrase, "because I am so very 'hands-on'" which signifies an attitude very much her own: the need of putting her innermost words and feelings (most of all love) into practice so that they would not remain as words and feelings without being transformed into deeds, even at the expense of great effort and sacrifice. Besides, as we have already seen, her director constantly motivated her toward sacrifice.

In this context of her life and psychological makeup, the desire to have the initials of her Lord and Master engraved upon her would be the most spontaneous and natural thing in the world, even outwardly, as a sign of her belonging to Him. Great was her desire to tell Jesus, "You are my Master. I am all Yours, to the point that I have engraved Your name upon my heart."

She submitted these desires under obedience to her spiritual director who, of course, denied her repeatedly until the day came when he not only suspected, but was convinced that this could be an inspiration from God for a soul of such soaring flights. He then gave her permission to have it take place on Sunday, January 14, 1894, the feast of the Holy Name of Jesus, and he promised her that he would entrust her to God in a very special way.

Conchita managed it very simply and naturally, as someone who was accomplishing a long cherished desire, without any dramatics or pretensions of heroism. She immediately felt an interior force that caused her to fall prostrate on the earth and her only exclamation was, "Jesus, Savior of all, save them, save them, save them!" She was not motivated in the slightest way by complacency, selfishness, or narcissism. She didn't even say to the Lord, "Now indeed have I been able to show You my love with something that is worthwhile." No, the interior force was entirely directed toward others: the salvation of all mankind and its redemption. It was like a reaffirmation and emphasis of that word that she had heard four years earlier, during her first spiritual exercises: *Your mission is that of saving souls.*

The temptation to dramatize — in one sense or another — a fact so out of the ordinary can be strong. Some do it in a way that is aberrant and abhorrent; others in the direction of heroic sacrifice. For Conchita, it was neither one nor the other. It was, certainly, an outburst of love — a frenzy for the cross — but executed with great simplicity, as a natural consequence of her burning love, framed within the context of her life.

I should not want it thought that this is a personal interpretation of the why and wherefore of such an important act — the monogram — in the life and journey of the Servant of God. As good as such an interpretation might be, it would be worth nothing if it were not in agreement with the words and deeds of Conchita herself.

Let us see it in her own words:

"I told [my director] the hunger that I had to be more of Jesus; that because I was so hands-on, I wanted him to give me permission to mark my chest with a monogram that would say, 'Jesus.'"

On January 14, 1902, eight years after the event, we read the oldest narrative that we have of it from the pages of her personal spiritual diary: "Eight years have passed since I branded my chest with the most holy Name of Jesus, JHS, and it has not been erased. With a divine motivation that was not my own, I asked for the salvation of men and at that moment, I was struck down by the supernatural passion of a thousand feelings of holy zeal rising up in my soul. Here is where the Apostolate of the Cross, that is to say the Works of the Cross, was founded with all that it entails.

"Oh, blessed hour that my heart so long ago desired with such immense ardor and secret and extraordinary impulse! My spirit longed to be of Jesus, completely of Jesus, even to marking my body indelibly in order to belong completely to Him.

"Obedience made me wait for this great joy for a long time, and upon achieving it… I was filled with such happiness at the contemplation of the red, and later the brown, characters that marked me with the coat of arms of my eternal Master. It seemed that I forgot myself, because a new, great and extraordinary feeling seized me and made me exclaim, in the midst of a most living faith and with the greatest emotion, 'Jesus, Savior of all, save them, save them!' It was remarkable that I had found the strength to outline, cut, and burn the letters. Upon feeling that weight on my soul of a greater need for other souls, of an infinite thirst for graces for the world, I could not contain myself; I fell to my knees and with my forehead in the dust, covered in I don't know what of the supernatural and holy, and with an intimate impetus of my soul, I cried out. I repeated something many times to heaven, something for which I felt an insatiable need, and that something was the salvation of souls!

"It seems that the Lord threw a veil on my understanding so that I would forget myself (my joy in already being more His) and left me only with that imperious necessity of asking, of crying out for others, of pleading for their remedy, their salvation, their happiness through Jesus, their Redeemer, their Savior, their Glorifier, their everything... and my everything... but I never imagined that this hour was 'the Lord's hour,' which He had been disposed to overflow with graces, with stupendous graces for the world!

"What a lowly instrument was used by the Lord! Eight years have passed and I have never tired either of being amazed or of giving thanks. Blessed be the Lord a thousand times! I have reflected today, being grateful for that blessed hour, and I have seen clearly how love of neighbor derives spontaneously from the true love of God, almost without our realizing it. Both of these came only from above, for humankind tends to the earth alone.

"How great God is! How small the creature! Truly, 'In the desire to lift up your head there is danger and in the desire to lower it there is security.' Each day, I am more convinced of this great truth. He is everything... I am nothing... and in knowing this, one encounters truth and peace of heart."

The importance of this act in Conchita's journey is not in what she did, but in her response to God, which can be described as most generous, superabundant and divine. Immediately afterward, torrents of graces overflow upon her like waterfalls from heaven and there is a dizzying ascent in the arms of the Lord. Human expressions of tenderness are incapable of expressing the outpourings of divine tenderness and the demands of Christ's love that hasten to purify her and despoil her from herself in order to unite her to Himself.

Betrothal

Within a few days, the Lord prepares her for the grace of mystical union: an analogy of the betrothal — the sixth dwelling. Her spiritual director suspects it and tells her so, and the Lord confirms it for her. Yet He does not want her to go blindly; the consequences were to be terribly painful, but enormously fruitful.

"Will you pass through everything?" He asks her repeatedly, and she responds, "What is this 'everything'?"

He invites her to accompany Him in the prayer of the Garden and offers Himself to place on her lips the chalice from which He had drunk. Later, He tells her, *"I invited you to accompany Me in the prayer of the Garden, for how could I unite Myself with you if you did not know the site?"* Meanwhile, her

27

director writes her a complete relinquishment to Jesus which she is to fulfill on the twenty-third of January, the day on which she receives the special grace.

Consequences

The effects of the grace of union and her complete surrender did not delay in manifesting themselves. The tenderness of the Lord returned upon her as in a truly loving pursuit.

"The Lord neither left me during the day nor during the night with that loving pursuit, with that divine invasion. The comparison is very poor, but just as when a suitor tries to win over a heart he does not leave half-done anything that he employs in obtaining the object of his affection, so the Lord... oh, unrivaled Sovereignty... it seems that He was driven toward the complete possession of this poor and miserable soul. I will not be able to describe the unlimited tenderness, the intimate attraction, the continuous calls, that made me ashamed and even to retreat far from the Tabernacle... sometimes I wanted to hide myself, to flee from His gaze that followed me in such a sweet and affectionate manner that it melted me as much as it confused me. I wanted to bury myself under the earth, to run to a corner, to a place where He would not find me... but it was in vain.... He always showed up, and so He would find joy in my pain, in my shame, in that embarrassment that His pursuit caused me.

"There in the sanctuary of Divine Love, He communicated to me in an indescribable manner and He told me, 'Drink from My Spirit so that it will be not only for you; these are too many graces for only one soul.' But what love, what tenderness, what sweet remarks the Lord then presented to me, how He gained my will, making me fall madly in love with Him, but with Him crucified! In what ways He began to speak to me of the cross.... As if He were opening before me a road seeded with sacrifice, crosses and all types of thorns, inviting me to travel it by His side!

"But the love of the Lord, of such great tenderness, is more demanding every day: *'You will have much to suffer for My cause, but will you let yourself be formed by the Will of My Father? Now it is as if you are on your honeymoon, but soon, very soon, sorrow will begin within you; aren't you My cross? You will give Me many souls, but they will cost you more than your own children. Entwine yourself more and more with Me... prepare yourself to suffer.... I will never abandon you, and if I test you, it will be in the measure of your strength; do not fear.'*

"He continued asking me about external things and concluded by asking me for my time... my thoughts... my affections ...my hours, my sleep, my eternity, my mother, my children, etc.... How He caused me to make my filial, conjugal, and maternal affections divine!

"*'Forget yourself,'* He told me. *'Do not look out for yourself, do not find yourself.... Do good deeds as if you weren't doing them, without even thinking of them after you have completed them. Take your pleasure in Me and do not plan but to please Me. You will reach Me, but in the cross and what is more, you will not find Me elsewhere. The cross will be lightened with charity towards your neighbor, with self-denial and with love for God: to the measure that these three things grow in your heart, the weight of the sacrifice will be diminished.'*"

I have purposely spent a great deal of time citing these

pieces of her writing, for it is a particularly important moment in Conchita's spiritual journey: the tender outpourings of her love for the Lord and the constant and growing demands of that love go hand in hand. That dizzying ascension toward the pinnacle of her life of union is realized in a short lapse of time — less than a month. They are the answer of the Lord to an act carried out by her with the utmost simplicity. She herself comments days later, "I had never suspected the transcendence of an act that I executed with simplicity, although with some resistance on the part of this donkey [her human nature]."

As a married woman

In the midst of all of these graces, it seemed that the Lord was pleased to emphasize His high goals regarding Conchita: to sanctify her as a married laywoman, without segregating her or setting her apart from her familial and social life.

The fourth of February 1894 (within that same, truly extraordinary month) was the Sunday of Carnival [the Sunday prior to Ash Wednesday]. Traditionally, on this day, a dance was organized for the community of San Luis Potosí. As the date approached, at the beginning of her prayer, the Lord told her, "*I want you to go to the dance.*" Conchita resisted, objecting that she would see things that she did not want to see, that He would be offended there, that she would let her imagination go wild, that she would not be able to pray. The Lord insisted, "*Precisely! I need someone who loves Me. Do not look at yourself. Did you not offer to do what I wanted? You shall never be separated from Me. Wherever you go, I will go. Give yourself totally to Me, so that I will give Myself totally to you.*"

Conchita notes in her diary, "At three o'clock in the morning I returned from the dance. I did many acts of love and reparation there...." Later on, she writes: "That which I did for You, Jesus, was very little... so many sins.... I felt them pierce through me like the swords that pierced through You. What vanity! Those temptations came so near to me. So many, many lies in that world of phantom joys! Such emptiness, my God! It seems impossible that such tinsel and lies can flatter! Last night, I more deeply understood what You are worth and the benefits that You have prepared for me. How much I owe You, Jesus!

"It seems that Jesus put the world and Himself in parallel, because I felt profound contempt for the world and a longing to reach out and unite myself more and more to Jesus with stronger bonds, with the cross. 'O, my God, who would ever be able to understand Your intentions? Who would believe, my Jesus, that a dance would bring my soul, finally, the ardent desires of the cross...?' I have resolved to embrace myself with it. It seems that upon taking my heart toward Him, He has placed these desires for sacrifice in it. Why have I risen so quickly to this step that my nature rejected yesterday? Ah! I feel that I am not myself, that grace drew me forth, that it did not let me delay for even a minute. Why this hurry, this succession of feelings that shout at me, 'Always higher; rise, rise, toward the cross'?"

And she concluded that paragraph of her diary, "Well, okay, my Jesus.... I want what You want: I will live where You wish, and I will die in You, the same within a convent as in the middle of a dance. Your Will shall be my will, although it may cost me, although blood may flow, it does not matter. I already know that You are everywhere and that nothing is an obstacle when You wish to communicate."

Conchita did not know what God's designs were, but accepted them beforehand; throughout her entire life, upon knowing the will of God, she would docilely and generously accept it.

The Symbol of the Cross

A few days later, Conchita saw the symbol of her life, of her spirituality and of her mission in the Church, in celestial splendor, as with the light of glory and in the manner of the ancient prophets.

First, she saw a dove among the splendors of light. At that time, she did not understand it as the symbol of the Holy Spirit. Right afterward, she saw a grand, glorious cross, with a heart in the center crosspiece. The heart was living, beating, encircled with thorns that punctured it and it was pierced by a lance and a small black cross was fixed to its center. It was all surrounded by flames, as if by living fire, and crowning it all, as if covering the great cross with extended wings, was a white dove, the symbol of the Holy Spirit.

The Lord Himself deigned to explain the symbol to her step by step: in order to scale the great cross to the Divine Heart that is at the center; to associate herself to the supreme mystery of Christ, Priest and Victim; to penetrate deeply into His Heart, surrounded and pierced by the thorns; to plunge herself into the sea of bitterness of His internal sorrows — those of His entire life, symbolized by the small black cross — in order to transform herself into Christ and offer herself with Him so that the Holy Spirit, Who is Love, may reign for the glory of the Father in the salvation of men. It is a sublime symbol, rich in meaning, of admirable unity and great relevance for our times.

Perhaps there has never before been so much suffering in the world and in mankind — pain caused by injustice, self-ishness and human limitations. To a great extent, it is wasted suffering, suffering without meaning. We know that Christ the Savior, through His cross, death, and resurrection came to transform suffering, giving it the meaning of salvation and redemption; that "it was necessary for Christ to suffer and thus enter into His glory" (Luke 24:26). What message is of greater relevance today than that of making use of so much suffering in mankind — the inevitable and the voluntary — so that, united to the sacrifice of Jesus, it might be transformed through the love of the Savior into an instrument of salvation and bear the fruits of eternal life?

Obviously, to believe in the saving fruitfulness of Christ's cross does not mean to stand idly by in the struggle against suffering caused by unjust situations, violence and misery that are the consequences of selfishness and sin — the sin of mankind and of the world. It indicates neither an alienating nor a conformist attitude. It is necessary to fight against sin and its consequences. But we know that suffering is inevitable — due to natural causes or through the selfishness of mankind — and we believe that the Savior came to transform it and to give it a divine meaning and transcendent fruitfulness. We want to make that divine meaning and that fruitfulness ours in order to live in the love of the Lord and our brothers and to extend the reign of God, Who is love. That is the message contained in the symbol that Conchita saw.

From then on, Conchita tried very hard to live out her own symbol, in hidden and quiet sacrifice, always within the

33

framework of her family life as a wife and a mother. For her, once seen, that vision began to draw back the veil that was hiding the plans of God.

The word of the Lord, which had been like a barely audible melody during her first spiritual exercises in 1889 — *"Your mission is that of saving souls"* — returned to resonate now in its full orchestration, as the principal theme of a concert: "Jesus, Savior of all mankind! Save them! Save them!" Her mission began to clearly delineate itself: The Lord promised her, *"You will found an earthly cloister"* and she envisioned long lines of nuns in habits. Her director wrote to her: "You will save many souls, but through the Apostolate of the Cross" and she was filled with abounding joy upon realizing that it will be not only she, but that there would be thousands of souls.

A few months later, on the third of May, the first cross was raised, just as she had seen it, and that same year the Apostolate of the Cross was established diocese-wide through the work of Bishop Ramón Ibarra González. The seed for the Congregation of the Sisters of the Cross of the Sacred Heart of Jesus had already been cast and it was initiated in 1897. The promises of the Lord began to be fulfilled.

A spiritual marriage

A new stretch in Conchita's path toward God — one of grace and of fruitfulness — began in the year 1897. She had been married for twelve years and was still nursing her seventh child. The union of her soul with Jesus had constantly grown.

Ever since the last months of 1896, she had begun to glimpse what the Lord was preparing for her: "I saw a vast countryside, I might almost say that its horizon was not distinguishable, and there in its depth there seemed to me a happiness, an eternal joy.... I heard what Jesus told me, *'Do you want to cross this road, My little daughter?'* I felt my nature resist, but without doubting, I responded, 'With You, yes, my Jesus.' *'Really?'* insisted the Lord. 'Yes, my Jesus, yes.' *'But see that it is sown with stumbling blocks, thorns and a lot of pain... yet in the end, there is true joy. It is the way of the cross.'*

"Later, I was asking Him how He could be served with my being trash and He told me, *'Trash is also burned and can communicate fire. You will communicate it.'*"

Repeatedly, the Lord invites her: *"Come closer. Tell Me that you want to be more My own."* She replies, "I do not know what to make of this, and I nearly tremble before a future of sufferings... and I only look at Him with all my soul...." The Lord responds, *"Who can love you as I have? Did I not tell you that I want you crucified? I want to possess you and you to possess Me. If you could only understand these words: 'to possess God.'"*

"And what can I do to reach this?" [Conchita asks]

"Look," He continued, *"generally, the possession of God in a soul and of a soul in God is according to the measure of purity in that soul. Be pure, with the purification of all of the virtues. Then you will possess God more and God will possess you more."*

He also said, *"Be at peace. Do you not see that when I ask something of you, I Myself give it to you? Correct yourself in what you see disorderly, but in peace, suffering without fuss or disturbance."*

The divine light causes her to become absorbed in the mysteries of God. Meditating on the beginning of the Gospel of Saint John, "In the beginning was the Word and the Word was with God and the Word was God," she feels her soul being overwhelmed in luminous and inexpressible immensities. Even the sole mention of the word "Word" makes her entire soul vibrate and shake with gratitude and love.

Her spiritual director orders her to resist those lofty experiences for eight days. She obeys and despite the fact that the interior impulse and the words of the Lord captivate her spirit, she wants to obey and comes to tell Him, "Do not speak to me of beginnings or of eternities. Wait for the eight days that my director told me. Let me obey." And the Lord tells her, *"Obey."*

On other occasions, Conchita had gone forth blindly, living the graces of the Lord step by step and responding to His invitations, but without knowing whence the designs of the Lord were leading. On this occasion, it was impossible not to see. The words of the Lord were clear and final:

"*'You were born for others. Rise and I will direct you.*

"*'Expand your soul. Receive Me. I want to possess you. Come nearer to Me. Purify yourself. I want you to try to love Me with perfect charity. Study all that this request of Mine embraces. Prepare yourself.*

"*'Receive My Word....'* And later, He told me: *'The Gospel is My Word. The Word is the Word of God. My daughter, the Word pursues you....'*

"*'How can this be?'* I responded. *'Am I not yet yours, entirely?'*

"*'I want,'* He continued, *'a heavenly betrothal with your soul. Purify yourself through the crucifixion. You are lacking much in order to arrive where I wish you to reach....'*

That same afternoon, the Lord asked her: *"'Do you consent to what I asked of you this morning? I need your will. I have loved you from the beginning of time. The Word became man for your love. Do not deny Me that which I ask of you.'* I experienced such shame and confusion and at the same time a strengthening of I don't know what divine feeling that was flowing over my soul and my body, that I went to my director as soon as I could, because I could scarcely dare to look at the Lord from pure embarrassment.

"My director thought that I should say yes to the Lord, although very, very humbly; that I should give myself to Him in whichever way would please Him; that I did not want to deceive or delude myself and that if this was not His will, I could take back my word.

"*'Truly, daughter, do you give yourself to Me with all of your will? Do you wish to be all Mine? Can I make use of you?'*

"'Yes, Jesus,' I answered Him, 'I will be all Yours without delay, helped by Your divine grace, because I see a mountain of crosses come upon me.' *'So now,'* He told me, *'it's My turn.'*

"'I am not worthy, Lord,' I told Him... but He answered me: *'Nobody is worthy of such a special grace.'* The Lord did not let me escape, I must say. Oh... and how would such an honor of God not move me, since He needs nothing from the most miserable of creatures?

"Then He told me: *'I have received your soul as My betrothed. In the beginning was the Word... and already I loved you. The Incarnation was the continuation of Eternal Love, of the Eternal Word, the mystery of union with man and for the possible union of man with divinity. You are My betrothed. Purify yourself.*

That which awaits you is very lofty. The Father and the Holy Spirit will be there.

"'Purity cannot unite with anything that is impure, or less pure, regarding that purification of which I have spoken to you. Behold, My daughter,' He told me, 'sanctity is not in one's state of life, although these may be steps, but in the purity of the soul. The soul that is purest is the one which draws closest to God, whatever its state on earth might be.

"'Don't you see the end to which I have been bringing you for some time? Did I not tell you, 'prepare yourself,' 'I want to possess you,' 'the Word is pursuing you,' 'purify yourself'?

"'For this I have let you have a glimpse of My greatness... My eternity... My immensity....

"'Behold, your betrothal will be with the Word, because I want to give you His same cross. You will be the spouse of the Crucified. Do you understand now?'"

Then, on the ninth of February 1897: "Jesus told me, *'Get up! The Father and the Holy Spirit are here. They have come because I want to introduce them to your soul as My betrothed.'* Oh, my Father, [her spiritual director] what mortification this causes me! Could this be possible? If you would see how ugly and horrible I see myself and how dirty and dreadful I am! If a prince of the earth, the most handsome, should love the most horrible monstrosity, this would be nothing compared with the difficult situation in which I am: wretched! I see myself and I meditate... and I suffer and I am saddened and even reject such a touching dignity. To me it seems nonsense, a madness, a mistake, an impossible thing in regard to Jesus. Oh, that the Lord will pardon me, my Father, but put yourself in my place and you will see what anguish this causes me and how much I long to be good and perfect.

"With that, I could do no less than throw myself to the ground, with my forehead there, humble and confused. Oh and of course, feeling the presence of the three Persons!

"Doubting, I told Jesus, 'I don't want to believe this; give me a sign that it will not cost You anything.' Jesus told me, *'Do you not know that your path is that of faith?'*

"On the following day, in prayer, I asked Jesus, 'Truly, my Lord, was last night real? Why did the Father and the Holy Spirit come? Are they not always with You and inseparable from You?'

"*'Certainly We are inseparable, but what I did for you was a special grace which you will never come to understand, nor be properly grateful for.'*"

Conchita rightly concluded, "I do not know what happened to me with this new fire that embraces my soul — a new fire that also has great potential to unite me with the Word without my asking for it! His charms and His memory sway me! They carry me! It seems to me that this is going to end in delirium… in madness…. What do I know, poor me? … I let it be done as He wishes! May He be blessed a thousand times!"

His Excellency, Bishop Martinez, Conchita's spiritual director for the last twelve years of her life, places this occasion, the grace of transformative union that uses the analogy of matrimony (the seventh dwelling), on February 9, 1897. Years later, upon reviewing the graces of the Lord in her life, she herself gives an account of the grace of spiritual matrimony and comments, "Would that I had known that they were not only betrothals...." Later, after receiving the central grace of her life from the Lord in 1906, upon asking the Lord if this was the grace of spiritual matrimony, the Lord answered her, *"It is more, for matrimony is a type of union that is mostly external."*

We do not know of another case in which the Lord has conceded this grace of transformative union to a married woman while her husband was still living. Regardless, it is something extraordinary and we can only recall the word of the Lord to Conchita, *"I allowed you to be married for My high purpose, for your good and that of many souls.... So that many may understand that marriage is compatible with sanctity and for other Most High purposes that I will keep to Myself."*

The preparation is begun

The various stages, or periods, that we distinguish in Conchita's life are our classification alone. They are points of reference. The spiritual journey is continuous and one grace is a point of departure for the next one.

The preparation for the central grace of her life, which she would not receive until March 1906, was initiated a short while after the signet grace that we have just mentioned. On the fourteenth of February, the Lord told her, *"Prepare yourself for the day on which My Church celebrates the Incarnation of the Divine Word; on that day, I came down to unite Myself with Mary, becoming flesh in her purest womb, to save the world. That day, I want to unite Myself spiritually with your soul and give it a new life, a divine and immortal life, in time and in eternity. Prepare yourself, purify yourself and cleanse yourself, because the benefit that is prepared for you is very great, very great."* He let her determine what this grace would really mean: "*...in this highest union that I wish for you, Jesus does not pass away but remains in a special manner in your soul. He remains forever, if your soul does not abandon Him.*

"*I descended to Mary's womb to suffer for you and I will descend to your heart so that you suffer for Me. The union with the Word will make you live with My own suffering and offer it toward the same end: the glory of My Father and the salvation of souls.*"

Conchita felt humbled before the magnitude of these divine favors and even said to the Lord, "If I think of myself... I figure that You have made a mistake. Go, Lord, and look for a holy soul, some pure spirit of a truly secluded and good consecrated woman. But to come to me, Jesus, with such very great graces...!

"Leave, Lord, do not lower Yourself, and do not touch me so that You dirty Your whiteness.... Tell me frankly, Jesus: don't I truly disgust or repel You? How can this be possible, when I find myself thus?

"'*Precisely,*' He answered me, '*because you find yourself disgusting, I do not find you so; herein, you have the secret of My affection.*'

"No, my Jesus, no! Do not tear me from my earth, from my nothingness! Let me be embraced by it. Don't You remember that You put this affection in my soul? Do not raise me up. No, Lord, do not lower Yourself, either. Look, we should stay in our places: You on Your throne and me on the earth contemplating You and enjoying seeing You happy.

"'*I already know that you are worth nothing and do not have your own merit, but indeed you have My merits, which are yours, and with these your soul appears beautiful to the eyes of the Father and the Holy Spirit. Do not be afraid.'"*

Conchita related all of this to her spiritual director and he "determined that in order to prepare myself for that which the Lord wanted of me, I should make a month-long retreat that would conclude on March 25. Each day would involve five hours of prayer [a good part of them during the night], all the while taking care not to neglect my obligations at home."

On the twenty-sixth of February she began this retreat in great affliction, with some humiliations that were not sought and others that were, with the difficulty of not being able to concentrate because of so many obligations. Nevertheless, there was a great deal of fervor and increased prayer and sacrifice: "I asked much of the Holy Spirit that He would direct and illuminate me during this retreat in order to achieve the fruit which I sought, which was to purify my soul to achieve that which Jesus wanted."

"To purify my soul to achieve that which Jesus wanted." Conchita wrote these words before beginning her days of retreat. She discerned that this was what the Lord wanted for her soul. Indeed, it happened that way. When a soul moves itself and breathes in that atmosphere of the lofty supernatural, God permits it to understand, through the medium of a kind of intuition or divine instinct, that which He wants. It is a superior light that does not take the darkness from the path of faith, yet nevertheless, makes the soul vibrate in unison with the Divine Plan.

There are yet many years until the central grace of her life occurred. She doesn't know it. She thinks that it will be immediate. Nevertheless, she realizes that the Lord does not just want her to prepare and purify herself, but also that He Himself will be in charge of that preparation. They are graces of burning thirst, of profound union and of painful purification that will prolong much further beyond the twenty-fifth of March of that year, for which she is preparing herself.

"My soul burns with the thirst for perfection, purity and sacrifice. My heart also burns with a tangible fire that makes it beat and puts color in my face."

The requirement of the Lord is intense: *"I want your life and your strength and every second to be employed in Me for my Works."*

"All day filled with God and drawn toward Him, I could say that my soul was in continuous prayer. I could feel my love toward the Word increasing...."

Conchita feels humbled by the light of the Lord and responds, "Who am I? As if it is I who could explain that which my soul feels upon seeing itself allowed to enter these depths?"

The Lord invites her to greater and greater docility: *"Let yourself be formed and let it be so with your director as well. You still need perfect abandonment to the Divine Will. The day on which you reach this, nothing on earth or in heaven will disturb you anymore."*

Quite rightly, the Lord asks her to allow herself to be formed, as it is a month of intense and harrowing purifications. She successively suffers the purifications of humility, faith, patience, fortitude, and penitence. She continues the purifications of will and of hope and enters the purification of charity. The page which we transcribe below is particularly strong and sorrowful:

"During my morning prayer and Mass, and later with equal or greater ferocity, I was accosted by a terrible temptation, or more accurately, by many temptations against the Church and its ministers, against the mystery of the Incarnation and against Jesus Himself. With them tearing at my heart, I have doubted the truthfulness of my director. It seemed to me that he was deluding me and that the Church was deluding me and deluding both of us. It terrifies me to even write this, but I had to tell the truth in order to judge where this great wretchedness of mine is capable of going.

"I felt, I repeat, that all spiritual, religious, and pious life is farce and fiction. That which we long for and for which we sacrifice ourselves is nothing — that everything is a lie, and with horror I have seen myself tempted to detest creation and to confront Him Who is Justice itself — to throw in His face the injustice of creating us for chaos! At other times, I have seen myself inclined to believe that God does not exist, and at others, that if He does exist, He is so grand and so independent that He is not concerned about His poor creatures.

"All of this: namely that God, the Word, descended into the womb of Mary seemed to me an aberration, and that it was an illusion that Jesus Christ has ever existed.

"I have seen myself angry, and even desperate, among a thousand battles, broken in pieces and alone — alone — because, doubting God and my director, then to whom shall I have recourse? Mary?! But if there were not Jesus, how would I think of Mary?

"Oh, my God, this must be skepticism, materialism, atheism. Unhappy and a thousand times unfortunate the poor heart that does not believe, that does not hope!

"I heard these words inside of me: '*Here you have the purging of hope.*' What a horrible martyrdom; I know of no equal, because without support or hope, the soul has to suffer an infernal agony. It does not know to be grateful, at least from my point of view, for the great benefit that God provides when one is able to believe and hope and love!"

Yet, Conchita concludes: "I believe, I believe and I hope against all hope. I love You and I want to love You, to love and to be Yours even amid the darkest night of my understanding."

Alternating between the graces of purification and of union, those days pass until the twenty-fourth of March, when she writes, "Today I am not able to say that I have entered into prayer twice again, because I have not left it since I awoke. Truly, I have placed my soul with my God." In profound absorption and prayer, she concludes her retreat: "I want nothing, nor do I ask for or look for anything. I see tomorrow coming, the day of the great promise, with a tranquility that amazes me, abandoned to the Divine Will, having the same peace whether I receive it or I remain in my own filth."

A painful test

The day for which she had prepared with such care arrived and nothing happened. In her personal diary we read: "I offered myself to Him eternally and I repeated to Him a thousand times that I loved Him, even though He might give me nothing. I purified my affection, making it disinterested and humbled, very humbled. I asked pardon of Him before all of heaven for my daring. He was silent and I was ashamed. My soul arose with a vehement attraction toward Jesus, but like the heavenly bodies, only from a certain distance, without being able to launch myself, drown myself, lose myself within Him. Inexpressible torment! Silent Jesus and also deaf, it seems. I who am nothing in His Divine Presence, hardly dare to look at Him. In silence my tears have flowed."

Conchita remains truly embarrassed and ashamed, thinking that it had all been her pride or arrogance for daring to expect such a great grace. Nevertheless, examining herself with every faithfulness, she comments: "Today, I have suffered much, so much. I do not believe that it is my pride, although perhaps I'm not aware of it, but indeed, I had to put almost all of the virtues into maximum practice, trampling myself, conquering myself, struggling."

For us, it is obvious that the previous purifications and the bitter sorrow caused by what she believed was her audacity were indeed preparation for the central grace of her life. The Lord had previously described it clearly, without any mistake. In light of many graces and subsequent events, we recognize it without a shadow of doubt. But she could not know that the time had not yet come and that she had barely begun the preparation that had to last for nine years.

This immense sorrow makes the sentiments of a most pure and detached love bloom in her soul and produces truly sublime pages: "I love You, my Lord, with my forehead in the dust and from the depths of my nothingness. I love You and I will love You, even if at the end of such suffering, Your Will would give me an eternal hell. This does not matter to my purest affection. I love You not for my own interest, but for You being Who You are, the Divine Word.

"You are right, yes, yes. How could You join Your purity

to a disgusting mud hole! Thus, each one in his place, Lord. You on Your throne, me in my trash heap. But today, receive this heart, even if crushed by the greatest, but most just and earned, humiliation. Receive, Lord, my affection, even though it is from one not worthy even to look at You.

"I will love You, Lord (at least this is what I feel), with all my soul, even when You do not return to give me consolation. I hope, with Your grace, to go on with my life without even the smallest change. For this, Lord, I ask that You humble me, to cure my pride.

"Yes, most beloved Jesus, I love You, even if You do not love me. I will follow You even though You despise me, even if You flee from me. I will not abandon You, even if You abandon me. I will sacrifice myself for You even if You condemn me. I will look to You always, always, and I will live nailed to You with my soul and my mind and everything that I am, though You might find me disgusting, even though You might never turn to look at me.

"Your insignificant puppy will always be at Your Divine Feet, quick to gratefully retrieve the smallest crumb from Your table. If You permit it, I firmly accept being a mangy and vile mutt, but with the unequaled honor of belonging to You. I ask only one thing of You, Jesus, and it is that You grant me the grace of never offending You; with this I will be happy, without striving for anything else."

How love grows in a soul that sincerely looks for God, when pain purifies it! The Lord, moved by such a pure and detached love — which is what He wanted — goes so far as to give her a balm. Without asking for anything, she heard, *"Can it be that I am not able to test you? I am the Master of giving and taking, of stretching or shortening, but I never deceive, because this cannot be a part of Me. Who would be able to penetrate My hidden judgments?"* Conchita did not dare to believe it and wrote, "It seems to me that I invented everything." A month later she heard, *"I do not deceive. You will see everything more clearly later."* On May 19, *"I do not deceive, nor am I able to deceive. Did I perhaps tell you the year?"* In this way, the Lord made her understand that He has His plans and His time and Conchita recovered her assurance, confidence and hope. Each year until the day of the Lord came, she prepared herself for the day on which the Church celebrates the Incarnation of the Divine Word.

I wanted to describe this moment in the journey of the Servant of God with sufficient detail because it is particularly important; besides connecting the previous graces with those following, it sheds light on all the others.

The last years of this stage of her life — that of her marriage — are a prolongation of the already initiated preparation of the Lord for the central grace, which continued in the first years of her widowhood. The graces of God, the instabilities of her life, and her great suffering fall within this preparation. Let us speak about each of these aspects.

The graces of God continue superabundantly, alternating with desolation and suffering. The formation of the perfect virtues that the Lord gives her merits a special emphasis.

From the time she was a young girl, Conchita frequently asked herself, "What is virtue?" with a great desire of practicing it. No one knew how to respond to her.

In this stage, the Lord dedicates Himself to teaching her the perfect virtues, as He had promised. He allows her to know about a great number of them. There is page after enlightening page of great subtlety and psychological astuteness. In each page the opposing vices and the ruses of the Malignant One [the Devil] are unmasked.

It is neither a theoretical nor a scholarly treatise, but rather, virtue incarnate in life, with great existential flavor. Nor is it perfection for its own sake. Each is called a perfect virtue because it configures one with Christ, the perfect model. There is humility, obedience, poverty, purity, etc., like Jesus Who was obedient until death, gentle and humble of heart. There is Jesus poor and Jesus a paragon of purity. There is Jesus Who possesses the plenitude of the gifts and fruits of the Holy Spirit.

In an outline of prefabricated spirituality, perhaps it might be surprising to have insisted here on the virtues that belong to a previous stage of mystical life. Let us not fall into confusion: perfect virtue is truly a gift, with the characteristics that distinguish it. It is no longer human effort that prevails; it is the action of God. These perfect virtues can be called the asceticism of the mystic: the obedience of the soul to the sovereign action of the Holy Spirit grows more and more according to the manner of the gifts, in the doctrine of St. Thomas Aquinas and other masters of the spiritual life. For this reason, the Lord's constant expression to Conchita is, *"Let yourself be formed. Do not resist,"* and other similar words.

The spiritual and perfect virtues are the divine means used to transform a soul into Jesus crucified. They are the preparation for the central grace.

Daily life: Upon reviewing this journey and knowing so many graces of her profound experience of God, we run the risk of forgetting that it is about a mother of a family who is submerged in her daily obligations. We run the risk of forming an image of Conchita outside of reality — idealized, made into an angel, or perhaps placed in another world, apart from ordinary life.

There is nothing more untrue. Her life — like that of all of us — had highs and lows. The divine honeymoon was interwoven with terrible desolation and abandonment. Her prayer life and intimacy with God were fully integrated with her obligations as wife and mother, which she fulfilled with great fidelity and self-denial. "All would be an illusion," she observes, "if I were not first to fulfill my obligations."

Her family life and the resulting social demands required endless sacrifices from her and constant rejection of what would be her pleasures, aspirations, and tendencies. She makes these sacrifices happily, convinced that it was not important to do what she wished, but to accomplish the Will of Him Whom she loved. She would not have done anything without securing the divine consent.

The Lord's graces, even though extraordinary, do not prevent her from turning herself over to the needs of her spouse and children, nor of accomplishing her daily obligations. The plan of God, of bringing her to a union and transformation in Christ, has to be realized in the equally demanding daily life of a secular woman, wife and mother.

She does not understand it, but she lives it. She fully accepts the Will of her Lord:

"Upon my asking Him why He was not saying these things to a nun, because they are so holy, and why He chose me, who am so awful that even thinking about it placed a thousand doubts in me, He said, *'I have My reasons that you do not know, and I am able to communicate with souls in all states; the world will receive an example of My power and many souls will be sanctified through this means.'* I understood that what the Lord wanted would be that, when I died or I did not know when, His goodness would shine upon a poor married woman, or better said, that His great power would be seen in all states of life. I am not able to explain more, and it has cost me great pain to give in. I do not wish to think about this, closing my eyes and walking, embracing the cross and doing that only through obedience. The only thing that consoles me is not feeling the least vanity in my soul. On the contrary, I feel only doubt, shame and pain."

The graces of God do not remove the painful effort of ascending step by step. The work of the Holy Spirit proceeds in her soul and her personal diary tells us of the constantly contrasting alternatives: a day of deepest prayer, followed by a dry and arid day "like a stone. Last night in heaven, and today… at a dance."

Nor is there any exemption from exterior difficulties and interior temptations: tendencies toward anger, temptations of despair, of shortening prayer. Sadness, tears, wounded ego, pain and illness. At times, the storms are tremendous.

The chisel of the Divine Sculptor does not rest:

"My body is also sick and I carry in myself three lives, each one stronger than the other: my family life, with its multiplied pain of a thousand types, that is, a mother's life; the life of the Works of the Cross with all of its pain and weight, that at times crushes me and it seems that I cannot bear it any longer;

my spiritual, or interior life, which is the heaviest of all with its ups and downs, its tempests and struggles, its light and its darkness, so that only the Lord can sustain me in it. Blessed be God for everything!"

The consequences of fruitfulness

Before finishing this stage, we ought to emphasize how each one of God's graces to Conchita has consequences of spiritual fruitfulness.

The grace of the sacrament of matrimony produced in her a great yearning for God and firm steps in her spiritual life with a great benefit for her husband, children, servants and entire family.

Her first spiritual exercises make these fruits so clearly tangible to her that from that time on, she practices them annually until her death. In fact, the inner word that she heard during that retreat "without any doubt" gives a strong thrust to her prayer life, to frequent and intimate communication with Jesus to the point of "walking continually in His Presence." It also stimulates her apostolic zeal.

Finding a spiritual director, a true grace of God, who helps her grow by giant steps and leads her to express her belonging to Jesus, her complete devotion and the grace of union, analogous to a betrothal, would result in the promise of a religious congregation, the implantation of the first Cross and the Apostolate of the same name.

This grace, or better yet, this collection of graces, analogous to matrimony, has its fertile fruit in the founding of the Sisters of the Cross of the Sacred Heart of Jesus at the beginning of 1897.

The Lord told her many times, *"You were born for others. I will give you many children that will cost you more than those from your marriage."* Her admirable pages about the perfect virtues that resemble those of Jesus will also be the fruit of this grace and the one that follows it.

This stage of her life — that of a married person — ends with the tremendous sorrow of her husband's death. Although she plainly accepts the Will of God, Conchita's suffering due to the death of her husband — the father of her children — is described with wrenching detail in her personal diary. We will not dwell on it, because it is already well documented in other publications. From the point of view of her spiritual journey, it is another element, and a very important one, regarding the already initiated preparation for her central grace. Its importance is revealed in the fact, at first a disconcerting one, that the Lord has asked her conscious and free acceptance of that great sacrifice beforehand. Conchita, overcoming her own tremendous pain, after a terrible struggle responds, clinging completely to the Will of God.

Conchita's prolonged widowhood (1901-1937) includes two clearly outlined stages in her spiritual journey:

The third stage, from the beginning of her widowhood until the death of Bishop Ibarra, spiritual director of the Servant of God (1901-1917).

The fourth stage, from 1917 until her holy death on March 3, 1937.

THE THIRD STAGE
(1903 - 1917)

THE CENTRAL GRACE

The first years of this stage extend the preparation for the central grace, initiated during the previous stage: a preparation containing great pain and suffering. Years later, the Lord permits her to understand, *"although a soul is never ready to merit it, you had to suffer a great deal before receiving it."* In effect, her personal diary lets us see with clarity the cumulative suffering in which she was immersed. In addition to the difficult blow she has received by the recent death of her husband and by her newly begun experience with the loneliness of being a widow, she has the task before her of educating and moving on with her eight children, some of whom are yet very young. The year 1902 is one of great desolation and silence from Jesus, accompanied by a prolonged illness that leaves her weakened and without strength for long months, twice at death's door.

"Son of Purity"

At the beginning of the year 1903, the Lord grants Conchita great enlightenment regarding the love of God that burns in her heart and prepares it for her encounter with Father Felix Rougier, to whom, from the first moment, she can speak of the love of God and of the cross with a passion uncommon to her, leaving him deeply impressed. Conchita's encounter with the Servant of God, Father Felix, is of incalculable importance for both of them because of the abundance of graces that the Lord wished to pour on them through their influence upon each other.

But the encounter with Father Felix also has as a consequence a multiplication of her suffering. Guided by obedience, Conchita has to leave her old spiritual director after having fought a thousand interior battles for months, without finding a way to connect the honesty that she wants and which is connatural to her, with her feeling of obligation to promised obedience and fidelity to him. She does not know what to do and fears disappointing the Lord by one or the other pathway. What an unheard of torment for the sensitivity of a soul that could conceive of no greater pain than that of offending God! The Congregation of the Sisters of the Cross, immensely loved by Conchita — the apple of her eye — was at the point of collapsing and disappearing. This was all accompanied by humiliation beyond belief, by slander and gossip against her. Her humiliation would grow deeper yet. Added to her other torments was the truly harrowing pain a mother feels at the loss of her youngest son, Pedro.

Conchita could hardly imagine that all of these sufferings would culminate in the realization of her mission. Yet even then, the Lord asks that, like Abraham, she voluntarily sacrifice Father Felix for Him.

In July 1904, Father Felix returns to France to speak with his Father General and by order of his superiors, he is prohibited all communication, direct or indirect, with the Servant of God, Conchita. She complies with this order with absolute fidelity, although with great sadness. In her personal diary she writes, "I am left alone, without a director."

Preparations

Although she does not know it, the influence of the Lord on her soul continues, preparing her for her central grace. In October 1904, she again offers everything to the Lord:

"The Works of the Cross are my life and a doorway that I see opened for Your glory.... It all seems slow to me next to the fire that my heart feels, but all of this tells me that there is something I have to get rid of and today I want to take care of it, crushing the impulsiveness of my desires, assisted by divine grace.

"Oh, my Jesus! If You want the work of the Priests of the Cross [Missionaries of the Holy Spirit] to remain as it is, in its beginnings, and that it never be established, I wish that as well.

"If You want them to turn against me, even those who are most able to help me, I want that as well. If You want them to consider me a dreamer, a hasty, gullible person without good judgment, I want that as well. If You want my soul to be embittered at seeing Your Work stagnate due to my lack of skill and my insufficient response, oh my Jesus, my soul aches, but... I want that as well. If You want me to live in the remorse of deceiving myself that what I suffer is a punishment for my sins and that thus I should live and die, nailed to that cross, I want that as well.

"I surrender, Jesus, to Your will. Here I am. I will be quiet. I will suffer in silence. I will obey. These three things I offer to

You today through the hands of Mary, giving You thanks for everything. I only wish not to offend You, my Jesus, nor ever to make You sad. No, my Jesus, even faced with death, I will let what pleases You be what pleases me and what You want be what I want."

Thus, we see clearly how everything is part of the prolonged preparation for her central grace.

As Father Felix stayed in Europe, the spiritual direction of the Servant of God remained in the hands of Father Emeterio Valverde y Téllez for a short time, followed quickly by Father Maximino Ruíz. Both became bishops later on, one of León and the other of Chiapas. Father Ruíz eventually became Auxiliary Bishop of México. These two priests, eminent for their knowledge and virtue, effectively helped her on her spiritual journey. It was during the spiritual direction of the latter that Conchita received her central grace.

These are her feelings upon beginning the year 1906:

"My spirit is in desolation. I have not forgotten to pray for the Works and the workers. How can I forget that which is my life? May the Lord permit this year to be the year of the Holy Spirit and of the triumphs of the cross. What does it matter if I should succumb to some kind of martyrdom, if it be for His glory? I feel myself propelled to greater perfection. What will Jesus want? I truly want to die to myself and to all that I desire. I want to place all of my love in that Heart of fire, filling myself solely with holy abandon in the arms of God. With all my soul, I have repeated to Him, 'Not what I want, my Jesus, but that which You want. Not how I want it, but how You want it. Not when I will it, but when You decide and determine it.' If it is Your will that I live and die with the martyrdom of desire, without ever seeing my hopes realized, it is also mine for being Yours, Jesus.

"Give me the ability to bring souls to You, Lord, especially those of my children. You see my suffering, You know my difficulties. Help me, Lord, to faithfully fulfill my obligations toward each and every one around me."

Her personal diary is a constant hymn of praise and thanksgiving throughout her suffering, always happily accepting the will of the Lord: "He is my all and His will is mine." Thus, the Lord Himself directs her path: *"You follow your path, which has already been set before you: humility, purity, simplicity and pain; this is your path. If you follow it, you will be holy."*

Conchita does not suspect the nearness of the grace that awaited her. She observes, however, "I am suffering a lot, but I love the cross — in whatever form — in order to be an emissary of the will of God. I clearly feel the Divine Architect shaping my soul. Continue Your work, Jesus. Do Your work in me. I will repeat it a thousand times; only help me and sustain me with Your grace. That is what You want. That is what I want."

During the month of March she prepares herself, as in previous years, for the day on which the Church celebrates the Incarnation of the Divine Word. In spite of being ill, she begins the retreat that Father Duarte, S.J., is preaching at the convent of the Sisters of the Cross. She senses that this retreat is especially important, not because she expects the actualization of the grace promised nine years before, but because the Lord is asking something of her: "I am on retreat. My Jesus has deigned to place on my soul a drive toward sacrifice, toward that something that He is asking of me and that I hope to have clarified.

"You are asking something of me, I feel it. I have told You

that You should take it, but if You want me to tear it from my own heart so that I can give it to You, I will do it, of course, if it is Your will. Today I want, and my heart shouts, GENEROSITY. Therefore, my Jesus, see that my soul aches, but if You want from this instant that I burn my heart as a holocaust here at Your feet, and do it for Your pleasure, then that will be my pleasure. I have asked You for life, as You told me one day, so that I can suffer more, but if you wish to cut it short, without my seeing the realization of my desires, without vows and without the Oasis [The Oasis, for Conchita, was the convent of the Sisters of the Cross. The Oasis is a place where graces of the Lord are poured out upon a dry spiritual world. The Sisters of the Cross, in the convent, care for the needs and desires of Jesus on behalf of an arid world which ignores and refuses Him], without a pile of straw or dung where I could die, without even knowing anything about the beloved foundation: cut it short, snap it, because it is worth nothing. My poor orphans... You and Mary will be their parents."

With this generous, or better yet, this heroic offering, Conchita prepares herself for what the Lord wants and He Himself confirms for her that those were His wishes: *"I want you to belong entirely to Me, so that all of your affections are for Me. I want this place where I rest — namely, your heart — to be cleansed of all dust."*

The Mystical Incarnation

March 25 comes "and thus, empty, I received Him in Communion [Communion was before the Mass]. I wanted to tell Him many things in the 'Incarnatus' and I did not even know when it happened.

"In the first memento [the memento of the living, during the Roman Canon] I felt the presence of Jesus joined to me. He told me, *'Here I am! I want to become mystically incarnate in your heart. I have fulfilled what I offered. I have come preparing you in a thousand ways and the moment of fulfilling My promise has arrived. Receive Me.'* I felt a joy mixed with indescribable shame. I thought that I had already received Him in Communion, but as if reading my mind, He continued, *'It is not that way. Today you have received Me in yet another way. I am taking possession of your heart... to never again separate Myself from you. Only sin will be able to separate Me from you. This is a very great grace that comes to you prepared by My goodness. Humble yourself and be grateful for it.'*

"'But Lord,' I dared to say to Him, 'was not what You had offered me a betrothal?'

"*'That has already taken place. This grace is infinitely greater.'*

"'Is it a spiritual marriage?'

"*'It is more, because marriage is a type of union that is more external; to become incarnate, to live and grow in your soul without ever leaving; for Me to possess you and for you to possess Me as if in one substance; without your giving life to Me, but rather I giving Myself to your soul in a compenetration that you cannot understand; this is the grace of graces.'*

"'Oh, my Lord,' Conchita tells Him, 'What if it is all imagination and lies?'

"*'You will know it by its after effects,'* He answered me. *'What fidelity I demand of you! To always carry Me in your soul! Nobody earns it. This type of union is very deep, is very intimate and if your soul is faithful to Me, it will be eternal. You believed that you were going to die and I gave you a new life. Breathe it in! It is pure. It is holy. It is the life of your Jesus. He Himself is Life, the Word that has loved you from all eternity and prepared this day for you.'*

"'Lord, Lord,' Conchita tells Him, 'would that I would humble myself and ask Mary to give thanks for me, so that I can imitate her telling You in my revolting unworthiness and nothingness: "Behold the handmaid of the Lord; be it done to me according to Your word."'"

I have wanted to narrate with accurate detail — although much is omitted — this event that I have referred to as the central grace in the spiritual journey of Conchita, because it is the key to the apex and point of convergence of all the graces of God in her life and in her mission. All that went before was preparation. All that follows, in the continuation of her mission until her death, are the consequences of that preparation. It is in a sense, the supreme grace in her path, although on the other hand it is not the culmination, but the beginning of a new and more powerful spiritual dynamism, as well as a more profound integration into the Church. It is the beginning of a new love and of new graces.

Conchita lived it, but did not understand it. Only over the years did the Lord reveal to her what the grace consisted of, the ends that He sought in granting it to her, the consequences for herself and for others, and the demands that it brought with it. In 1897, the Lord had described the grace that He promised her with great clarity: *"I wish to unite Myself spiritually with your soul and give you a new life, a divine and immortal life in time and in eternity. Prepare yourself, purify yourself, cleanse yourself, because*

64

the good that is being prepared for you is very great. In this highest union that I offer to you, Jesus does not pass through, but instead remains forever in your soul in a very special way, if you do not abandon Him. I descended to Mary's womb to suffer for you and I will descend to your heart so that you suffer for Me. The union with the Word will make you live with My own pain and offer it to the same end: the glory of My Father and the salvation of souls." It is amazing to see how, having written it in her personal diary with such clarity nine years earlier, so much time could have transpired before living it and beginning to understand it. Such are the plans and times of the Lord for His highest purposes of mercy! For us, it is a solid guarantee of authenticity: things happen to Conchita only when the Lord wishes, not when she wants them, or when they could be foreseen by the human mind.

It is impossible for me to give a complete idea of the central grace given to Conchita, including its abundant, deep, and rich theological implications. Neither would the brevity of these pages allow it. It will undoubtedly be an object of in-depth study in the future. Nevertheless, I will try to give a synthesis of what it is, its ends and its consequences, unifying the elements that the Lord continues to give His Servant little by little.

"This Mystical Incarnation is an imitation of that which was brought about in Mary, but an imitation in the divine sense, through the same Divinity. It is a unitive, transformative and mutually penetrative grace, in which the Most Holy Trinity takes part, for it is a participation in the fruitfulness of the Father that the Holy Spirit achieves in order to make a Jesus out of the soul. It is the union of the Word Incarnate with a soul in order to reproduce the mystery of Christ, taking a creature as an instrument of sacrifice and immolation, making it a victim in union with Jesus and associating it

to the redemption in order to accomplish His plans of love."

Therefore, as far as an analogy is possible of the immensely great with the infinitesimally small and of the original with the imitation, we will be able to say that in the real Incarnation in Mary, the Divine Word took possession of human nature and united it to Himself in a unity of person. In Jesus, there is only one person: the Divine Person. In the Mystical Incarnation, God takes possession of a human person and unites her to Himself, not in a personal order, but in a dynamic one, with the dynamism of love. Love unites, transforms, understands, affectionately identifies, in such a manner that, without repressing the personality, the person wants only to love like Jesus, to feel and to act like Him, and to offer herself to the Father, suffering like Him, associating intimately with the crucified Redeemer and reproducing His image.

The Lord goes on to reveal to Conchita that such a grace is a *"free and loving gift that does not pass away, but is permanent, as long as you are united to the Word until you die. May you always be able to grow. You have a lot to pass through, that absorbs all love in One Love. His love and His suffering will be that of a mother,"* as an imitation and in participation with the maternal love of Mary. From then on, He frequently repeats that she should imitate Mary.

His Goals

Her understanding grows when the Lord allows her a glimpse of the goals that He intends upon giving her that grace; they are *"the goals of charity for My glory and for the good of many.*

"For this you should offer Me to the Father, crucify Me to the

Father.... All your life should be wrapped in love, in the fire of charity; in the measure that this grows, it will be easy to sacrifice Me, because the same excess of maternal love, communicated through the paternity of the Father with the Word, will allow you to enter into His goal of redemption, and so you may sacrifice Me as He sacrificed Me, that is, with and through an immense love. The Word became flesh and was mystically incarnated solely in order to be crucified; and that is the goal — that of the descent of the Word — because only by descending could He be crucified. The world was drowning in an abyss, and your Word overcame that abyss by coming to your heart in the Mystical Incarnation, and more than anything, by being constantly crucified on an altar, not of stone, but of the Living Temple of the Holy Spirit, through a priest and a victim that, by an inconceivable grace, has received the Father's love of participation. The Father wants Me to unite with your soul as Victim, allowing you to sacrifice and offer sacrifice with your own love, for the benefit of the world, which needs an upheaval, and the grace of human nature to turn itself around, to embrace the Cross and to be saved.

"*Moreover, in order to support this weight, you should divinize yourself. In life and affection you must live very high above the earth and you will keep your eyes on what is holiest and the most supernatural. Thus, you will possess Me more; thus, the worldly in you will disappear: that is to say, loving souls as My Father loved Me and sacrificing yourself in union with your Word, forgetting yourself. What a powerful Mediator you have in your Word in favor of souls! Understand this: the only Mediator is One — the heavenly and unique Mediator that can bring about salvation.*

"*Now do you see My redemptive plans in the Mystical Incarnation? Fulfill your mission without vacillating, daughter. Do not waste a minute, for in sacrificing yourself, you sacrifice Me; in crucifying yourself, you crucify Me; offer Me and offer yourself, but only under these stated conditions."*

Its Consequences

The consequences of this grace — according to the Word of the Lord — are endless:

"'It has many derivatives that you will begin seeing and understanding; thousands of graces for you and for others are derived from it.'

"Such a benefit crushes me, does not let me breathe, I will say, driving me to the foundation of hell. I want to hide myself, even from You." She feels shame and embarrassment and "a new-found humility," while at the same time she is "full of holy joy, peace and unspeakable well-being."

On the one hand, this new-found humility carries her to an immense, constantly expressed gratitude for these divine favors, while on the other hand, it keeps her always vigilant, distrustful of the ruses caused by pride and vanity and with a fear of self-delusion. She reproaches herself many times, above all on the anniversary of the grace, for not having sufficiently taken charge of the received favor and also for having neglected it. Only the targeted direction of His Excellency Luis Martínez, during the final stage of her life, helps her to free herself of fears and tethers in order to completely live the central grace of her life.

No wonder Conchita was afraid upon feeling her smallness before the divine favors and the consequences which the Lord let her discover continually. She realized that she was the "sanctuary and tabernacle of the Lord, the Cross of Jesus, altar and sacrificial Host, Priest and Victim." Her sorrows, derived from the same grace as priestly sorrows, obligated her to "absolute transformation into Jesus in order to offer Him" — and to offer herself with Him — and to be able to repeat in all the actions of her life: *"this is My Body... this is My Blood,"* mystically consecrating her entire life in the way in which the priest consecrates the bread and wine on the altar.

The Second Vatican Council has familiarized us with these concepts by explaining the doctrine regarding the spiritual priesthood of the People of God, a true mystical priesthood; at that time, however, the idea could be taken as quite bold. How could she not tremble on understanding the Lord? *"From the time of the Mystical Incarnation, a union between the two exists, such as you see. My offenses are yours and yours are Mine, but together we forgive... together we hope... together we sacrifice ourselves."* How could she not feel insignificant before the words of the Lord? *"I want you to be in Me as I am in you. Through the Mystical Incarnation of the Highest Priest in you, you are the Mother of priests. The altars are consecrated and you are such as they. I want to use you for the good of others, in favor of My Church. One of the ends of this grace in you is the martyrdom of love for the absence of the Beloved."* There are many words — too many to put into writing. For that reason, she herself comments, "I am not surprised regarding my rare mission on the earth," and her mission as a secular woman "as a poor married woman" — as Conchita says of herself.

These heights of union with God through her transformation in Christ leave us surprised, perhaps with a sensation of dizziness and disbelief. Undoubtedly, the Lord allows Conchita — and us — to see that those incredible graces are encountered as a seed, in embryonic form, in the grace of baptism: *"Upon placing the seal of the Holy Spirit upon your soul, I gave you the Mystical Incarnation on the day of your baptism. This grace was developing without your understanding until coming to its culmination; later on reviewing My life in you and clarifying the ideal that I had in your soul, transforming you into Me."* Moreover, the grace of baptism, that began the path, is for all. This sublime grace carries the spiritual priesthood of the People of God — of all Christians — to completeness.

The Mystical Incarnation is, therefore, a grace of transformation and identification with Christ in a dynamic order: a conscious and loving order. It therefore requires free acceptance on the part of the person.

Its seed is in the same grace of baptism through which, by the conscious and free acceptance of the faith and love of the Savior, the Word is truly conceived. Saint Augustine had already expressed it in relation to the Mother of God, who "through the greatest good fortune carried Christ in her heart, not just her flesh." The Mystical Incarnation is brought to fullness by the grace of baptism.

The identification with Jesus crucified is at the culmination of that grace; the result is making the soul co-redeemer with Christ. We will see how the consequences of this grace in Conchita were spiritual fruitfulness and maternity and how the sacrifice of the Cross is the supreme act through which Christ, Highest and Eternal Priest, completes His priestly offering. That spiritual maternity will always have a priestly feel that will constantly grow. It is the progressive transformation into Christ, Priest and Victim. *"Upon becoming mystically incarnate in your heart, I complete My goal: transforming you into Me, into sorrow — My Passion. You must live My life and you already know that the Word became flesh in order to suffer, not as the Word, but in My human nature and in My Most Holy Soul. The mother gives life to her child and I will give life to your soul, but painfully. This union, for the most part, will be one of pain, assimilating you with Me, if you allow Me to do it. A painful course awaits you in this intimate union; go through it without hesitating, for the Holy Spirit will be your strength."*

Chain of Love

The consequences of the grace of Mystical Incarnation are not slow in coming. Only two days later, on March 27, the Lord tells her*: *"You must forget yourself, throw yourself into My arms and offer it all, day and night, for the salvation and perfection of souls. You see, you are going to make a chain: each hour of your life is going to be a golden link, being offered with that intention; I wish that it not be broken until your death and this will be your own self-examination....*

"Give yourself to souls as I gave Myself, so you can assimilate yourself with Me. And how did I give Myself? With love, with sacrifice and without interruption. This is the way I wish your life to be in the future. I want more. I will choose souls that continue these golden hours that I wish you to begin without interruption."

"How can I go forward," Conchita asks Him, "if I am ashamed of being the worst?"

"It is not you, but I with you. After you, thousands will wrap

---

* Note: The expression "the Lord tells her" doesn't mean that Conchita heard those words with her ears or even her imagination. Rather, as she often explains it to her spiritual director, it is as if they were imprinted upon her soul.

themselves in the cross and its wounds and will give Me glory."

He clarifies this even further: *"Give yourself to Me with all of your possessions; throw yourself into My arms and live My life of Victim; notice that today I am not just saying live My life, but also My life as Victim, not only obediently, but abandoned totally to My will. The pinnacle is abandonment to My will — forgetting yourself and your surroundings (in this sense) trusting in Me, the soul drowning itself within My will and My power, adoring that which I do or do not do, dead in the paternal arms of an unlimited confidence. In this regard, the three theological virtues are exercised in their highest form — believing in My power, trusting in My will and dying within My Love."*

This Chain of Love — this Golden Chain — is the immediate result and living out of Conchita's central grace: as Jesus, Who did not live for Himself, but for the glory of the Father in the salvation of humankind.

Even more, the Lord deigned to show her how to concretely live that Chain, giving her fourteen rules with the characteristic virtues that the people who participated with her were to live. Her spiritual director ordered Conchita to begin immediately to practice one of these fourteen rules each week.

Spiritual Priesthood

A little while later, the Lord allowed her to see the necessity — and the incredible richness — of living the Chain of Love with a totally priestly sense — offering the Divine Word and offering herself with Him: *"In a certain sense, My daughter, you are the altar and the priest at the same time. Therefore, you have the sacrosanct Victim of Calvary and of the Eucharist with you,*

Whom you are able to offer constantly to the eternal Father for the salvation of the world. Upon becoming mystically incarnate in your heart, I have brought about this precious fruit of great favor in you. I have given you the greatest thing of heaven and earth — My very Self — but with this goal... alone... what would you be able to do? But with Me and in union with Me, many thousands of souls can continue saving mankind through the merits of that same Word. You possess nothing by yourself, but with Me, you possess all things. Now, do you understand the reason for the previous grace?

"*You are My altar and you will also be My victim; offer yourself in union with Me and offer Me to the eternal Father every minute with the noble goal of saving souls and of giving Him glory. Forget everything else, even yourself. You have a sublime mission, the mission of the High Priest... having Me in your heart, never leaving you. Millions of souls will unite themselves to this new energy out of My goodness, and My Heart will find solace; My Church will find help; My Father will find glory, and the Holy Spirit will find souls!*"

This Is My Body...

The Lord allowed more than two years to pass so that Conchita could assimilate and live these teachings regarding the Chain, offering the Word and herself with Him. They were two years of desolation and pain, of fear of having deceived herself in various matters. She did not let even a day go by without imploring the Lord regarding the founding of the Congregation of the Religious of the Cross (the branch for men), complement to the Works of the Cross. She did not yet suspect that there were still two other Works of the Cross.

In February 1909 the Lord showed her, with even more explicit words, the practical form of living the spiritual or mystical priesthood:

"My daughter, I want you to say these words often and above all in your sorrow, with a loving will: **'This is My Body; this is My Blood,'** *offering yourself to the eternal Father in union with Me. Do you not recall that you are host and must be victim?*

"With this union, I live in you, My poor creature; offer yourself so as to live My same life, giving yourself to souls as I gave Myself, for the same cause and with the same goal, that is to say, the glory of My Father and the salvation of the world. I with you, have created a society so intimate, that only in heaven will you understand it. I have united you to the redemption, to My redemptive and universal plans, giving you part of My sorrows for the good of souls.

"Do not fear, since I am with you, just continuing My plans regarding your soul. Let yourself be transformed, in Me, for the glory of the eternal Father. I do no more than continue My goal of the Mystical Incarnation through you. Offer yourself. Offer yourself and offer Me... so that you live, not your life, but Mine.

"That is the mission of the priest, which you must carry out: that of saying, **'This is My Body; this is My Blood.'** *It is not that it be of their own, but of Mine in union with them, Mine in their transformation into Me. For upon My being offered, it is not the poor creature through himself or in himself that is offered, it is I on his lips, it is I in his heart, in his body and in his blood, and it is for that reason that the sacrifice — that offering — is pleasing to My Father and obtains graces.*

"Your role is that of a priest and for that reason, I became flesh, was born, and live, beating in your heart, so that you could be so, offering Me in union with you, offering yourself in union with

Me, for the same goals of charity, through the hands of Mary, first priest and victim in union with Me.

"This, really, is the continuation of the Golden Chain; this alone opens the treasures of heaven and the souls of the Cross will multiply their links, fulfilling My plans of forming victims in union with Me who can say, **'This is My Body, this is My Blood,'** to the eternal Father through that powerful, transformative and intimate union with the Word.

"The Chain, therefore, is a priesthood of victim-souls who are united to Me entirely, absolutely, who are innocent and pure, who live My life of Victim, abandoned to My will for the benefit of the guilty.

"Souls are drowning, daughter, and it is necessary to save them. Plead for their salvation; again ask the Eternal Father to save them. With Me, say, **'This is My Body; this is My Blood,'** so that your children will repeat these same redemptive words. I promise you that heaven will open upon hearing them from pure and loving hearts… from souls and bodies abandoned to My will.… Repeat them with the intention of voluntary sacrifice, uniting all that you are through Him Who is, in Him Who is, anticipating in you all the future sacrifices of your children without end, as I repeated them from before you existed and My Father already accepted them. But understand, that when I offer My Body and My Blood, I offered along with it not only My physical body, but also My Mystical Body… in My Church and in souls, and with it My Soul and My Divinity, that is, the Incarnate Word, through which your sacrifices, and those of your children, will have worth.

"Thus, with your body and your blood, offer your soul, your heart, your abilities and your senses, your life and your death and the Works and the souls of your children… and based on your union *with Me, offer the Church, priests, all the just and sinners and My very self with all of them... always, daughter, always, for this is your spiritual mission on earth."*

From the preceding paragraphs, it is very clear that the Lord wanted to make Conchita a prophetic sign in His Church. The doctrine regarding the spiritual priesthood of the People of God, so clear and explicit, is written here more than fifty years before the Second Vatican Council, which highlighted the importance of the priesthood of the faithful.

In the previous stage, we have already seen how the graces that the Lord gave to Conchita had the immediate repercussion of spiritual fruitfulness. When dealing with her central grace this is even more true. The effects are multiple.

In the first place there is the nearness, the enthusiasm, and the involvement in the Works of the Cross of Bishop Ramón Ibarra y González, Archbishop of Puebla. The relationship between the two is that of two holy souls (his cause of beatification has already been introduced). They both receive a new impetus toward sanctity by their influence upon each other. The Lord brought him to her as a son and gave him the name "son of consolation." Bishop Ibarra accepted that affiliation and, at the same time, that of becoming the spiritual director of the Venerable Servant of God. By special concession on the part of His Holiness, Pope Pius X, he would become the first to take vows as a Missionary of the Holy Spirit, without leaving his archdiocese.

Conchita daily asked the Lord for the greatly desired and difficult foundation of the Missionaries of the Holy Spirit as the crowning glory of the Works of the Cross. The Lord gave her three foundations:

In 1909, the Covenant of Love with the Sacred Heart of Jesus for lay people who aspire to the perfection of Christian life and who, in their homes, wish to carry out a holy and exemplary life filled by the spirit of the Cross: *"I wish that the spirit of the Cross be renewed... that sacrifice be embraced and that the richness of suffering that is rejected by the world be known and appreciated, since this is the only way to be saved. What I wish is that the Holy Spirit possess all souls.... Those souls, daughter, will be especially loved by My Heart, which wishes to make Itself felt and loved in Its internal sufferings.*

"And I am going to tell you something," the Lord continued, *"You will also be the mother of that covenant... you, a humble instrument of My goodness, whom I have wanted to serve Me for My glory."*

In 1912, the Apostolic League [now called "The Fraternity of Christ the Priest"] for bishops and priests wishing to live the spirit of the Cross, committed to extending the reign and devotion to the Holy Spirit, to living the mystery of Christ, Priest and Victim, and to spreading and to preaching the Cross, that is the Gospel, and to helping the Works of the Cross.

In 1914, the Missionaries of the Holy Spirit, founded after a thousand battles and due to the insistent petitioning of the archbishops of México, Puebla and Linares.

Before the founding of the Missionaries of the Holy Spirit, when the archbishops were negotiating permission for the aforementioned founding before the Holy See, His Holiness Pope Pius X wanted to examine the life and writings of Conchita. She was advised to submit an excerpt of her *Life* and *Diary*, and with great embarrassment and sacrifice, she complied. In 1909, she wrote nine volumes, which were an impressive synthesis of her life up to that point, sending all of it to the Holy See. No significant detail was omitted. She wanted to submit the entire manuscript, with the greatest loyalty and transparency, to the judgment of the Church. In her diary, Conchita comments, "If Rome says that I am only a dreamer, then I will undoubtedly believe it."

Prior to this, by order of Bishop Alarcón, Archbishop of México, her spirit and writings had already been examined by three priests he had appointed. All three were experts in theology and men of knowledge and virtue.

As a result of the closeness of Bishop Ibarra to the Works of the Cross, he considered it prudent to propose a new examination. The Archbishop of México was in agreement and designated Fathers Cepeda, Ipiña, Daydí and Mayer — all of them highly qualified. With great shame and embarrassment, Conchita unconditionally submitted herself to the dispositions of ecclesiastic authority. She observed, "If these things are not of the Lord, then let's turn the page," always disposed to obey the voice of the Church.

Additionally, Bishop Ibarra had the foresight to send an abundant collection of writings about the Mystical Incarnation and its antecedents to Father Poulain, S.J., author of various books about mystical theology, and considered a preeminent authority in that field. That wise act had excellent results, since Father Poulain's response was received in Rome at the most opportune moment. Having managed to have the Servant of God in the Eternal City [Rome] at that very moment, he asked Bishop Sbarretti, a future cardinal, to personally interview Conchita. As a result of this long interview, many prejudices and misunderstandings were cleared up. Bishop Sbarretti was very favorably impressed by the virtue of the Servant of God and by the authenticity of her spirit. The Lord had already announced to Conchita, *"You will go into a place of combat, but My Work will triumph."*

In 1925, when Conchita told Bishop Martinez of all of these examinations, she told him, with characteristic humor, "so many, many examinations… and when will the distribution of awards be?"

On October 2, 1912, through the special concession of Pope Pius X obtained by Bishop Ibarra, Conchita took her vows as a religious of the Cross with overwhelming joy. But these vows were valid only for the hour of her death. Meanwhile, she would continue her family life and the mission that the Lord had entrusted to her as a lay woman. That same day, Bishop Ibarra, the holy Archbishop of Puebla, accepted being entrusted with the spiritual direction of the Servant of God, which he would continue until his death.

In the Holy Land

In 1913, a great Mexican pilgrimage to the Holy Land and Rome was organized and led by Bishop Ibarra. Among the pilgrims were Conchita and two of her children. This pilgrimage has importance in her spiritual journey because, in addition to the joy and the grace of meeting with His Holiness Pius X six times — one of which was a personal interview — the journey through places where Jesus had lived had great significance at that point in her own journey.

The Lord had allowed her to understand what one of the goals of the Mystical Incarnation was: *"to outline My life in its various phases in you."* Conchita did not know how or when, but the journey through Palestine bearing as it did the living experience of the presence of Jesus in her soul was, for her, an intense and profound experience of the diverse phases of the life of Christ and its mystery. Bethlehem, Jordan, Mt. Tabor, the Sea of Tiberias, Jacob's well, the Holy Sepulcher in Jerusalem, the Garden of Olives, and above all, Calvary and Nazareth, were not only interesting historical points of reflections for Conchita, but also a current reality as she traversed with Jesus the stages of His life, carrying Him present in her heart.

Upon entering the grotto of the Incarnation in Nazareth and seeing the inscription "Here the Word was made Flesh," her soul vibrated to its depths and the divine light and intimacy with Mary penetrated her deeply. Even the fact that she walked those places in the company of the holy archbishop had significance, as the Lord allowed her to discover a little while later.

"Son of Solace"

Although brief (a little more than four years), the spiritual direction of Bishop Ibarra and his relatively frequent contacts with the Servant of God was a grace for both of them. Their influence upon each other was laden with the fruits of sanctity.

For Bishop Ibarra, it was the final stage in his transformation in Jesus and preparation for his holy death as a victim for the Church. For Conchita, the prelate was, above all, a solid support in his relationship with the Works of the Cross; he helped her to confront especially difficult moments on her path, enlivening and deepening the love and intimacy in her soul with the Most Holy Virgin, thus providing an effective impetus to the unity of her life in God.

During her retreat of 1912, directed by Bishop Ibarra, Conchita writes, "During no other retreat did you give me such an impetus. The words of the Lord were, '*Onward, My daughter! Do not waste time. Ascend through these struggles for perfection; propel yourself with love, and through love, you will be able to do it all. God never inspires the impossible. Walk already obeying, whether you are in the light or in the dark, having the Divine Will as your North Star and holy obedience as your guide.*'"

Her prayer was, "Holy mother, give me your sentiments, your humility and that abandonment to the Divine Will as when you pronounced those divine words that will form my life as the fruit of these holy exercises: 'Behold the handmaid of the Lord.'"

At that time, the Lord gives Conchita abundant understanding regarding unity in the Holy Trinity, in the Church and in the life of the Spirit. He permitted her to see that moment of her life as *"one step closer to unity"*; that not encountering rest except in God is a sign of His divine Presence; that the apparent absences are *"filled with hunger"* for that which God communicates abundantly; that her soul should be like a very clean mirror in which God is reflected, so that her life can be an intimate and constant relationship with the Trinity.

The Lord also tells her that the steps of transformation are not perceptible to the human senses, but are nevertheless indeed real; that *"this step crucifies and kills"*; that *"this new stage will be painful, for the most part, but also one of great blessings"*; that she has encountered the path that He Himself has opened to her and which He wished her to follow.

At the same time, the Lord reproaches her for not having made use of the great resource that she has — namely, the

Mystical Incarnation. She has placed it in a corner.

It is truly admirable how the Lord takes care to lovingly form her, outlining her path and preparing her for the stage that would follow: the most painful, but also the most dynamic and the most spiritually fruitful, through a great and very profound integration into the Church.

On December 25, 1914, the day after the founding of the Missionaries of the Holy Spirit, Conchita writes, "Finally, that most desired day came, the day long-awaited with prayers and tears, with penances and sighs, with blood and deceptions, with bitternesses and accusations, with rejections and slanders, difficulties and oppositions! The Work of God has continued through all this, so that it has triumphed and has been canonically founded. My God, Virgin Mary, thank you, thank you!"

The Works of the Cross had by then already reached their culmination, thanks to the effort, determination and sacrifice of the holy Archbishop of Puebla and the painful sacrifices of Conchita.

The virtuous prelate had at that time only two more years to live. At the end of 1916, the ailing Bishop Ibarra took residence in an apartment located on the upper floor of the house of the Servant of God, in order to be healed and to recover. During his painful illness, until his exemplary death on February 1, 1917, she tended to him with almost maternal care. The Lord would later tell her that just as Mary offered Him up in the temple, He wanted, *"on the day that the Church celebrates the Presentation"* that she offer Him a son — the child of solace!

The Central Grace

He Represented Me at Your Side

In Conchita's spiritual diary, there are many pages in which the Lord clarifies for her the importance of that particularly painful moment caused by the death of Bishop Ibarra, whom Conchita always refers to as "my Father." It is the end of one stage and the beginning of the last stage of her itinerary.

Let us see one of these pages.

"My daughter, the son of solace that I gave to you after the Mystical Incarnation visibly represented Me. I allowed you many opportunities to understand and I told you how My life would continue in you, allowing you to pass through its various phases from the Incarnation up to Calvary.

"I led you to his side, so that you would always remember Me through him, to retrace the steps of My life in Palestine, the sites in which I was on the earth: Bethlehem, Nazareth (where I spoke to you often), Jordan, the Garden, the Cenacle, Calvary, the Sepulchre and others. That Jerusalem, so full of My memories, the mount of the Ascension, where My Blessed Mother lived and died.... In Tiberias, I told you some things alluding to that which was happening to you and that you do not remember. I saw you on that lake, in a boat, at his feet, representing Me and remembering Me. Do you remember it?

"I told you how you would see the blood of the one who represented Me flowing out without martyrdom. I announced his death to you: that I wanted to bury him in My Heart.

"I let you see and understand how you would see him die and be battered in the waves of a sea of pain, drowning in it and that you would remain alone on this side, in the world, alone again with the weight of the Works of the Cross.

"*Likening himself to Me, you saw him humbled, persecuted, slandered, suffering incomparable torture for souls, burning in devotion, without the power to do more than pray and sacrifice himself. You saw him in your own home gushing out blood and dying like a victim at your side and offering you as well as a victim to the eternal Father.*

"*And on the day — for the Church that of the Purification — of which I had told you that it would be your day and that on it you should offer the sacrifice of a son, you saw him die, obeying My Will, offering him to Me on the altar of your soul, sacrificing him for My approval.*

"*I told you that you would take him to the sepulchre, imitating Mary. After seeing that act, which broke your maternal heart, I told you to remember Mary as she returned from Calvary when the sun went down, imitating her in your heart.*

"*It was a great honor for him to represent Me at your side and in various ways. I purified him in a thousand ways, in order later to finally nail him to the cross upon which he died. That soul responded to My Will, offering himself as a victim in My union, and he is safe.*

"*My daughter, you have entered into the path of solitude in relation to the Mystical Incarnation, as I have explained to you before.... It remains for you to traverse the last stage of your life imitating My Mother in her solitude, in order to strengthen your union with Me, your adherence to My Will, and your desires for heaven. You are alone, but with the pain of solitude like Mary and by imitating her, you will give life to innumerable children.*"

THE FOURTH STAGE
(1917 - 1937)

SOLITUDE AND FRUITFULNESS
IN THE CHURCH

The last stage of the spiritual journey of the Servant of God consists of the final twenty years of her life and as we shall see, is the consequence of her central grace.

We already saw how the Lord announced to her and planned this final stage in her journey: of union with Mary, in the mystery of her solitude, imitating her when in the greater part of her pain, but with great favors; of the prolonged absence of Jesus, with a feeling of association and of fruitfulness with Him; of having more than enough, with a hunger for God.

Upon reviewing the pages of Conchita's diary, we see how, from the earliest months, the lines of the divine program continue to appear. His Will is clearly manifested to her. It teaches her and prepares her, letting her experience a painful participation in the salvific mystery and He takes charge of the effectiveness of its fruitful consequences for the Church, the priests and the Works of the Cross.

The Solitude of the Mother of God

Almost immediately, the Lord began to uncover that aspect of the mystery of Mary that Conchita had to imitate and live, with great enlightenment about the solitude of the Most Holy Virgin and of her spiritual maternity: *"For these last times set aside for the reign of the Holy Spirit, it is reserved to honor the suffering of the solitude of Mary, His Most Beloved Spouse; suffering in which only the virtue and fortitude of the Divine Spirit could sustain her with life.*

"Mary lived as if miraculously and only in order to purchase the graces that her maternity demanded for humanity. She lived in order to be an instrument of the Holy Spirit in the fledgling Church. She lived in order to give the first nourishment to that Church and to earn from her children the heavenly titles of Consoler, Protector and Refuge of Sinners.

"That stage of Mary's life is almost ignored, being the source of bitterness for her heart, the quintessence of martyrdom, the purification of her love. For the world, it's the inexhaustible fountain of grace and of mercies. At the foot of the cross, her children were born. My death gave them life in the heart of Mary, but she, before dying, had to manifest that maternity on earth, purchasing infinite present and future graces for her children with the cruel sorrow of My absence.

"Mary won the special halo as Mother of Humanity with her martyrdom of solitude after My death. By chance, does the world know, appreciate and give thanks for this? But now the time has come that these children will be her children and for their happiness, will honor that broken heart, with its sharpest, most significant sacrifices. Thus, Mary purchased millions of graces for each and

every one of them and it is time for them to be grateful to her.

"How wonderful Mary is and how forgotten in those years of her cruelest suffering, during which she gave the life of grace to her new children! My making her Mother at the foot of the Cross was accomplished so that they might be born by virtue of My prolific Word. There, at the foot of the cross, they were only just born; but did the mission of a Mother, much less that of Mary, the Mother of Mercies, end there? No, daughter, there on Calvary her maternal mission had hardly begun. It needed years and years of enormous martyrdoms to purchase each and every one of the graces for all mankind until the end of time.

"This has been almost ignored by her children for centuries and centuries. Thus it has been with Mary. A veil has always covered her virtues and her life. Now that the reign of the Holy Spirit is going to be renewed, as in a new Pentecost, Mary will shine again. This Most Beloved Spouse of the Holy Spirit will come to light, so that her praises are sung at the same time as those of that divine Spirit and will continue to be an instrument of the operation of graces which are extraordinary for their abundance, and by which they are going to spill out over the world. A powerful response is awaited from the earth through these two means: the Holy Spirit and Mary. Mary will shine with a new sparkle before guilty humanity, winning over many hearts with an aspect or color no less than that of her martyrdom of solitude.

"The Holy Spirit is the One Who today raises this veil that covered the most sorrowful period in the life of Mary. Many saints have announced a new surge of love for Mary and a greater knowledge of her virtues during these end times, and it is a very great grace that I have chosen the Works of the Cross for this purpose."

Later on, the Lord drew back even further the veil that hid the mystery of Mary's solitude in its unfathomable depth:

"My daughter, you have understood the first solitude of Mary — that is, her external solitude — but you have not thought about her interior solitude, the cruelest and most bitter, the heart-breaking solitude in which the spirit agonizes and is a prey to helplessness. Mary's martyrdom after My Ascension was not only for lack of My physical presence, but also because she suffered the most enormous trials of helplessness; like My own on the cross, the Eternal Father united her trials to Mine, which purchased so many graces.

"Mary, immaculate and without sin, had nothing to atone for and undoubtedly suffered more than any other creature, but her suffering, like Mine, was not to purify her, but to ask for forgiveness and to expiate the sins of others. It was for the purification for her children. At what hour did Mary's heart earn these graces? During the martyrdom of her helpless solitude, not from men, nor from My physical presence because, given her great living faith and perfection, she was consoled with the Eucharist. She earned them with her spiritual abandonment, the divine abandonment of the Trinity, which was hidden from her.

"Most souls ignore the martyrdoms of Mary's heart, abandoned by heaven, which she suffered through the years that passed after My Ascension. These were her trials, these infinite abysses of pain, and so much greater was her desolation since she had enjoyed My divine and human presence for so many years, from the highest union with the Trinity, from the first instant of her being. Mary suffered more than all the helpless souls, because she suffered a reflection of My abandonment on the cross, as I told you, and that has no comparison nor human language, to express it. Her martyrdom was of love and the helplessness that enveloped her for

so many years was a loving act of My Father, so that it would be pleasing through her, and that, through her, He wanted to shower the treasures and the seas of His graces upon souls.

"The echo of My internal Passion beat constantly within Mary's heart from that which had oppressed My soul ever since the Incarnation and was made known in the Garden of Gethsemane for a brief moment. During My life, although Mary knew, read and reflected My internal pain within her, My filial love always veiled it, so that she would suffer less. But after My Ascension, these martyrdoms wounded her with all of their intensity and bitterness, spilling out of her pure soul for the good of her children, until the end of the world.

"How much humankind owes to Mary and how these bitter pains are not known, honored, or appreciated!"

Conchita's Path: In Union with Mary

The Lord gave to Conchita this divine enlightenment about the mystery of Mary's solitude, her pain and helplessness in union with Jesus, and the secret of her spiritual maternity, not only so that she, as well as her children, would meditate, contemplate and give thanks for them; it was also to indicate that from that time on until her death, her path should be in union with Mary, imitating her and participating in the solitude of the Most Holy Virgin, as a reflection of her spiritual maternity.

After the death of Archbishop Ibarra, the first spiritual exercises of the Servant of God were undertaken in an "asylum of solitude." The one who directed this retreat was Father Felix Rougier and he oriented it, in its entirety, to living with Mary. In order to give Conchita this first push into her new stage, the

Lord had prepared Father Felix with his formation in the Society of Mary and his unblemished love for the Mother of God.

Numerous expressions have allowed us to see that Conchita very clearly understood the Lord's will for her during this stretch of road that had to last until her death: *"On this retreat I want to unite you to Mary, hope of the afflicted and if you truly are her daughter, you will fly with her through the paths that await you. She is the Mother of holy hope: exercise this precious theological virtue like her; the virtue of hope is the virtue of solitude and pain, the virtue that looks toward heaven and that makes the heart expand itself to possess it.*

"Each time that Mary, My Most Holy Mother, felt the pain of My absence in whatever form (and that was continually) she later offered Me to the Father for the salvation of the world and for the fledgling Church. That apostolate of suffering in her — that is, of the cross — during the time of her solitude, was the most fruitful and caused heaven to flood her with graces. It is the same with you: you have begun a reflection of the life of Mary in this new stage of your life and it falls to you to imitate her without wasting your pain, so that in her union and Mine, it will have value. Thus, in this form, make your pain of solitude supernatural, so that it is fruitful and to the benefit of your children. Behold, the souls that unite themselves with Me on earth through purity, sacrifice and love are those that achieve the most graces in heaven and even on earth before leaving for their homeland.

"Although you have your very extensive circle of saved souls, in imitation of Mary, offer Me and offer the one who represented Me with you, for the salvation of the world and the Works of the Cross. May all your pains have this purpose: the glory of God and the extension and perfection of the Works of the Cross.

"In My life for souls, My daughter, My Mother is never sepa-
rated from Me: that is, the imitation of our lives on earth has to be
simultaneous, although hers was founded on Mine. Moreover, just
as I was the Redeemer, she was the Co-Redeemer and the souls
that love her more and that make themselves more like her are those
that most perfectly take on My likeness.

"You, as a reflection of her life and of her sorrows, ought to
make yourself like her in this adherence to My will, which crushes
and pierces your heart. As Mary did, you have to win the crown
which you once saw, the maternal prize, the title which I have given
you, although with innumerable sorrows. You have to buy on earth
all the graces for the present and future children of the Works of
the Cross.

"Continue, in her likeness, purchasing graces for your children
until your death, accepting those martyrdoms of your soul which
My goodness has placed upon you, imitating Mary, and at her side,
learning to suffer for My glory."

Then, after the Lord had allowed her to understand the
deepest mystery of Mary's solitude — the martyrdom of helplessness — as a reflection of the helplessness which Jesus suffered in the Garden and on the cross, He told her, *"Imitate her*
in your smallness, even though by yourself alone you could never
reach that high. Pursue the imitation of her with all of the strength
of your heart, because you must do this in order to purchase graces
and purify yourself.

"The Father loved Me as He has loved nobody else. He loved
My Mother with infinite preference. It is a great honor when He
chooses souls to support redemption and co-redemption in union
with Me and with Mary. In this same way, the Apostolate of the

Cross is portrayed in its most sublime degree; that is to say, in innocent suffering, in loving and pure suffering, in redeeming suffering for the salvation of the world.

"The suffering that is united to Mine has this quality or virtue: the seed of divine fertility that obtains benefits for others. This suffering has the gift of multiplying itself, for everything in God, or that which comes from His divinity, is infinite.

"Advance, letting yourself be done and undone by God and men, very much united with Mary and although you do not see Me, although you do not feel Me, proceed on your path. If I clarify these points for you, it is because of your weakness. I intend to strengthen you. I will not abandon you. Trust and wait. Yes, daughter, lift up your heart to hope and, most especially, exercise the theological virtues during this stage of your spirit, in union with Mary.

"Behold, My daughter! My Most Holy Mother continued offering Me even after My death, offering herself, in union with Me, to the Eternal Father for the salvation of the world, for sinners, for the fledgling Church and for all of the needs of her children. She was the Co-Redeemer and she had to accomplish her maternal mission on earth. You, as a reflection of her and through her example, imitate her in her virtues and unite yourself to Me with her for the benefit of the Works which I have entrusted to you."

Generous Response

With the help of grace and by requesting the Most Blessed Virgin to help her and take her by the hand, the intentions of God regarding her journey, mission, and the Will of the Lord — so clearly expressed by Him and perceived by Conchita — receive a pure and generous response from her.

"The goal that I perceive in these exercises — forgetting myself, not looking to myself for my own interest — 'Oh, my God, deign to give it to me!' This pain kills me, but in order to imitate Mary, in order to make me more like her and more like Jesus, I do not want it to stop. I do not want to be consoled, for Jesus had no consolation. I do not want to be treated better than Jesus, my Model, nor than Mary, my Mother. If the Works of the Cross are strengthened by suffering and martyrdom and they grow, then may thousands of sufferings drown me in their waves, because that is the medium through which God will be glorified and I insist that all of my life glorify Him in everything."

The tone with which she describes that pain of loneliness is full of anguish. The understanding with which she accepts the sorrows of loneliness is even more amazing: "It is the action of God that is purifying me. The Lord tells me that He wants to make me like Mary in this way. It is a new type of martyrdom, something like the divine, not human; it is a mystery, but it is real in its effects: a vacuum, a sorrow without name, intense, devastating, although very much in agreement with the Divine Will. It is a spiritual sadness, piercing the soul which, without relief, without hope, wants solitude and flees from it; it wants silence and is slain by it; it looks for consolation and does not encounter it, not even in God, nor in His creatures, nor in the elements, nor in anything! Its life is the Will of God alone and at least with this colt (* Colt is one of many self-disparaging terms by which Conchita refers to herself) in this torment produced by that same Will that she loves, it looks only to heaven, yearns only for the Father and is sustained only by the company of Mary. Oh, what a rare stage for the soul!

"I have suffered much — so much — but embracing Jesus

close to my chest and contemplating Mary, with my heart shattered, I repeated to Him, 'Behold the handmaid of the Lord.' Cut and tear apart my soul with these martyrdoms that only You see... that the world must ignore. Rekindle them to the end that You want, only to give You glory; only to imitate Mary; only to purchase graces and vocations in union with Your merits."

The following invocation to the Most Blessed Virgin arose from the most profound depths of Conchita's soul: "Oh, Sorrowful Mother, because you know what grief is, because you weep with any heart that weeps and are the cause of its happiness! Have mercy on me and come today to be my companion, my sister, my friend and my mother!"

Several months later, she writes, "Mother, I weep on account of this terrible abandonment! You know, Mother of my soul, what it is to have God and not to feel God. I did not know that together with solitude, you also suffered helplessness. I feel compassion for you, Mary, and dripping with blood, my heart shouts to you, without breath, without support. Mother of the hopeless, queen of the martyrs of love, have compassion, have mercy on your very small, miserable child who wants to be good and cannot. Come to her aid, because she longs to suffer in union with you."

To the Lord Conchita says, "Oh, God of my heart, I cannot go to You without You! I want to be faithful to You, deny myself, love You and do Your will!"

In the Solitude of the Summit

These entreaties that spring from the heart allow us to discern that the circumstances of Conchita's life during this time were such that she not only effectively accepted the Will of the Lord, but that she also truly lived the life of solitude desired and foretold by Him.

Two of her children had already left home to consecrate themselves to God in the religious life. Both were generously offered to the Lord by the Servant of God, but the separation was very painful. Manuel, raised by his mother in the love of the cross, offers the sacrifice to God of never returning to his country or to his family. His superiors are in agreement and Conchita completely accepts this in the midst of her sorrow. Her other children are separated from her, one by one, upon marrying. Those of her siblings who have not died live far away.

Her humiliation, lack of understanding and shame are multiplied. Her feeling of helplessness in assisting her children in all of their needs grows. Her illnesses are frequent, even to the point of once finding herself at death's very door. Her spiritual director, now a bishop, is in a distant diocese and communication with him could not be frequent, even by mail.

For the Works of the Cross, which have been her life, she can do nothing. For the sake of prudence and to comply with the dispositions of her superiors, she keeps herself almost totally removed from the Missionaries of the Holy Spirit. She feels herself a nuisance in every way: among her friends, in her family and even among the Sisters of the Cross of the Sacred Heart of Jesus.

"God is purifying me; I understand that. He places bitterness even in the sweetest things. I find thorns everywhere, slights, scorn, public humiliation. My heart, which looks for companionship, affection, warmth and all such comforts, is rejected by those whom it most loves. My heart is humbled and isolated. Thank you, my Jesus! You and only You are and want to be my Only One. May You be Blessed!"

Upon reading Conchita's diary of this period, one cannot but feel a soul crushed by so much suffering. Day after day, there is very painful suffering. Some of her most profound suffering she cannot even dare to commit to paper and it remains a secret between God and herself.

If we add to this the most painful sorrows — the prolonged absences of Jesus, the ever more vivid suffering for offenses to God through the sins of mankind, the interior desolation, the terrible helplessness — we can have a vague image of how the Lord is cultivating her soul.

Spontaneously, the words of Saint John of the Cross come to mind:

> In solitude did she live
> And in solitude she had already set her nest
> In solitude does He guide her
> Alone, her beloved
> Also by loving solitude wounded.

At times, Conchita saw with great clarity that this stage of solitude was the attainment of the Lord's plans and of His graces: "There, when at the beginning He spoke to me, He once said, *'If you want to unite yourself to Me, you must drink from a chalice — and I do not deceive you — that is most bitter, but I Myself will place it to your lips. Do you wish to follow Me in this manner?'* Clearly I told Him that I would; but He did not place that chalice on my lips one time, but many, and never like now.

My heart hurts. May He be praised."

Sometimes, the Lord Himself allowed her to see the succession of His graces, especially in relation to the Mystical Incarnation: "Once in a while in this path of obscurity, solitude and thorns, You give me a ray of light... a breath of consolation to continue on with my life...."

"In 1905, I announced a special internal suffering to you, suffering that would break the deepest, the finest, the most delicate and intimate of human sentiments: a saving suffering; do you remember? And I added: it hurt Me to crucify you, but I must wound you, without compassion, in the deepest part of your soul, in the most substantial part of My cross, in the love of divinely inspired spiritual maternity.

"You see, My daughter, the first thing that I told you at the beginning of the Mystical Incarnation was that you should offer Me as a holy Victim on the altar of your heart to the eternal Father for the benefit of the world in expiation for sins, and yourself in union with Me. Later, I asked you to reinforce that offering through your union and compenetration with Me, saying in union with Me, 'This is My Body; this is My Blood'; offering Me up and offering yourself to the Eternal Father to obtain graces for the world. Now, I am telling you that you should do all of this in union with Mary and with her very heart. These are the three stages that the Mystical Incarnation goes through. What have you asked of Me but the martyrdom of love? That is the goal of the Mystical Incarnation: the martyrdom of love due to the absence of the beloved; the 'I am dying because I do not die'; that soul, losing itself in unity, absorbed in the Will and the solitude of God.

"My daughter, I am simplifying you in unity, so as to unite

you more to God. This step is very painful, but necessary. This purification in the most delicate part of your soul will be indispensable in order for you to receive the graces that will follow if you do not put up any voluntary obstacle; however, the benefits of these graces are incomparable. Abandon yourself to My Will, with Mary and in Mary!"

In this way, the Lord prepared the development and complete blossoming of Conchita's central grace, so as to give it a greater dynamism for fruitfulness in the Church.

Enlightened by the Lord and with the guidance of her spiritual directors, Conchita had certainly been experiencing the central grace of her life, humbled and profoundly grateful to her Incarnate Word. Embarrassment, humility, distrust of herself, and the fear of being deceived held her as if fettered, however, without bringing her to their ultimate consequences.

"After I learned that a cardinal had not liked all this about the Mystical Incarnation," she tells the Lord, "I experienced a kind of feeling of horror.

"Sometimes it seems to me that it is I who invents what the Lord says, or that I exaggerate, following my imagination and circumstances. But when I see that it is happening and I feel all its effects and that predictions are coming true in me, I am dumbfounded and I can only humbly say, 'I am the servant of the Lord. Why does He not get tired of such great wretchedness as mine?'"

The Lord also made her understand: *"Instead of pondering your unworthiness and losing time on this, figuring out if all of this regarding the Mystical Incarnation is or is not pride, say often and with profound humility, 'I am the handmaid of the Lord, let it be done to me according to Your Word.' Let this be your favorite short prayer and I promise you will have peace."*

Only during the last years of her life, under the direction of Bishop Luis María Martínez, would she feel free to thoroughly accept that central grace with all of its consequences.

In truth, the first to clearly see the need for taking away these bonds was Father J. Guadalupe Treviño, M. Sp.S., during the spiritual exercises of the Servant of God which took place in 1921. Upon summarizing the reflections that the priest had made during the retreat, Conchita wrote, "I must fully accept the Mystical Incarnation and its consequences. It is foolish humility not to recognize it and not to benefit from its graces. That the Lord willed to shed His graces upon a pigsty is not my concern. It is all His.

"Notwithstanding my great misery, lack of response and many defects, He continues His plan in me, because this is His pleasure. He looked for my littleness and was stuck with me and I cannot help but consider this truth: graces are measured according to the generosity of the Giver. He Who gives them to me is God, inexhaustible in mercy, power and love! My God, what can I do with this immense weight of Your favor and of my misery? The priest told me, 'Confidence in God, self-denial, complete abandonment in His Divine Hands.' One must see the abyss of God's mercy in oneself, even if it makes one dizzy. To abandon myself in God, Who abandons me. This is the degree of perfection that the Lord expects of me.

"I must let myself be loved by God to the point which He desires. I lack audacity and boldness. I get stuck in one place. I stop and I do not allow God to do His work in me, to follow the

101

course of His designs. 'Once and for all,' the priest said, 'finish with your confusion, fear and distrust.' By God's grace, I have seen the light at this retreat. I have dealt with the obstacle that was holding me back."

The "Son of Light"

The orientation of Bishop Martínez during the years that he was Conchita's spiritual director, up to the death of the Servant of God, follows this same theme.

According to his first letter in 1923, from which Conchita copied some passages in her diary, she writes: "I must simplify myself and fix my spirit and my heart on the grace of the Mystical Incarnation. That is the grace that will sanctify me and allow the designs of God in me to be fulfilled. I must meditate upon this grace, love it, be grateful for it and live it, to enter fully and without shyness into this divine world which this grace opens up for me. The aim of this grace is to make me a priest, a victim and an altar. Through this Mystical Priesthood that must be my constant occupation, my soul participates in that love of the Father that must be the Supreme Love. I must love with maternal love that Christ which I must offer up constantly in my soul. I must not waver.

"Is this too lofty? Well, it is natural that it be that way, because it is something which relates to God.

"That I am very small? All the better! This is what the Lord searches for and needs in order to realize great marvels: that His instruments experience their own lowliness.

"He says it is only natural that I feel embarrassment, because it always accompanies love and especially this spectacular love that God asks of me: motherly love; but this embarrassment must be very subtle and very divine, so as not to impede me, but rather impel me to accomplish God's designs. I must be mother as the Blessed Mother was, so that with her, I may be a priest."

Then, in another letter from the same year, Conchita extracts: "I must believe, with absolute steadiness, in the Lord's graces and especially in the Great Grace. I must let this most genuine and maternal love grow without obstacle... grow even to madness. If it is an excess, it must be a divine madness, which the Lord desires with His Sovereign Will.

"I must work to respond to the graces of God, especially in supporting the inspirations of the Holy Spirit with a loving docility, yet remaining in the truth, not attributing my misery to that which is God's work."

Bishop Martínez's spiritual direction to Conchita formally began with the spiritual exercises he directed for her in 1925, in which she gave him an account of the graces she had received from God, giving him a marvelous summary.

This spiritual direction, which took place largely through the yearly spiritual retreat and through written correspondence, was considered a very great grace from God by both of them. The "son of light," the name the Lord gave him because of the great wisdom he had in understanding and guiding Conchita, was a very strong support for her during this last and decisive stage of her life. Possibly nobody else was able to understand her better, and his accurate direction of great nobility and loftiness, helped her unravel the most fruitful divine treasures contained in the Great Grace.

The support of this great spiritual director did not suppress the sorrow and suffering of the Servant of God during this painful stage, but helped her to give them a full sense of ecclesial fruitfulness and to follow this path with certainty until its end.

Conchita was also a channel and instrument of the Lord's graces for the "son of light" and through the written correspondence, one can clearly perceive their mutual influence taking each other to their union with God. In the pre-preparatory session of the process for the beatification of the Servant of God, Bishop Martínez clearly expressed that she was one of the greatest mystics that the Church has ever had.

The dynamism of Conchita's central grace during this stage of solitude, greatly painful and admirably fruitful, led her to a full insertion into the priestly and ecclesiastical field.

From the beginning, certainly, priests had been a matter of deep concern and sacrifice for Conchita. From the first volume of her diary, this concern appears constantly. There may not be any among the sixty-six volumes where she does not mention this explicitly. Since Bishop Ibarra's time, both he and the Servant of God offered themselves as victims for the Church. In 1914, the Lord asked for the establishment and spreading of Sunday communion on behalf of priests. The Works of the Cross are eminently priestly. It is not a new interest, but the full blossoming of Conchita's mission. This is clearly manifest in the priestly message. In the years 1927 to 1930, there are more than a thousand pages of confidences to priests in her diary, in which the Lord urges priests to work on their transformation into Himself. To be able to realize Jesus's work — this is the mission of priests — it is necessary that they be Jesus. These are admirable pages, full of light and fire, about the life, the dignity and the saintliness of the priest and also about the dangers and miseries of priesthood, written with infinite respect and love. This is a case without parallel in the history of Christian spirituality!

But above all, is the sacrifice on behalf of the Church for priests. The Lord had said earlier: *"Through the Mystical Incarnation of the High Priest in your soul, I have made you mother of priests."* Bishop Martínez's guidance leads her to fully live that motherhood. Several times the Lord tells her, *"You are not your own master. You belong to My Church. You belong to My priests. Offer up everything for them."* Conchita, renewing her complete surrender to the Lord many, many times, says to the Lord: "I desire to belong to your priests forever."

The simple mention of the central themes of each of these spiritual exercises given to Conchita by Bishop Martínez, makes us see the enlightenment that God gave to him, so as to be able to unravel the consequences of the Central Grace. One can see how every one of the themes is related to the Central Grace, examining the various aspects and the richness of its divine implications in the wonderful unity of the Mystical Incarnation.

In chronological order, the themes are the following:

Your life in God: 1925
To love with the Holy Spirit: 1926;
To be Mother;
To be Jesus and Jesus crucified: 1928;
The interior of the Divine Heart of Jesus: 1929;
The consummation in unity: 1930;

The Third Love: 1931-1932;
The reposes of Jesus: 1933;
Divine intimacy;
Handing Jesus over to be crucified: 1934;
To live the Mystical Incarnation and its
    consequences: 1935;
The perfect joy: The consummation of charity.
    Joy in the midst of sorrow: 1936

Notwithstanding the great importance and the profundity of these themes and of the priestly message they convey, it is not possible to elaborate upon them. They exceed the limits of a few conferences and the scope of these lines. A great part of this material has already been printed and I refer the reader to those publications. The priestly message has been published by La Cruz under the title, *To My Priests*. Concar, A.C., has published a pamphlet by Fr. Roberto de la Rosa M.Sp.S., entitled *In Favor of Your Beloved Church*, about the mission of the Venerable Servant of God on behalf of priests. Several books by Bishop Martinez have been published by J.G. Trevino, M.Sp.S., which contain most of the spiritual exercises given to Conchita.

For many years, Conchita cherished the dream of joining the Congregation of the Sisters of the Cross, her daughters, and spending at least the last days of her life in the cloister after all her children had married.

In 1924, she consulted Bishop Martínez about this dreamed desire and she wrote down his answer: "He believes I am not supposed to enter there." Six years later, she again set the same consideration before him, this time not as a question, but urgently petitioning his authorization to accomplish it. Her director stood firm in his response, in spite of the tears of the Servant of God: "No, Conchita, this is not God's will." Conchita surrendered to the Divine Will and made a complete surrender to the Lord, one of triumphant love, by which she definitively renounced this long-cherished dream, only to please Him, and accepted herself as remaining at the door of the Oasis (the convent of the Sisters of the Cross) like a hotel sign-post or a guard dog.

The Lord granted the saintly director an abundant wisdom to clearly see that this was not Conchita's mission and this was the reason for his steadfastness. Many times she had heard the voice that said to her, *"You married because of My lofty designs...."* In God's plan, Conchita would realize her mission in the Church as a laywoman until the last day of her life.

At the end of 1935, a little less than a year before her death, the Lord asked from her and gave to her a crusade of souls that offer themselves up to God on behalf of the holiness of homes *"as a crowning of the Mystical Incarnation."* They must be persons, married or widowed, of proven virtue. The crusade was started immediately with the help of her director. Without making noise, in the silence of sacrifice, how many graces of faith, love and sanctity have poured down upon families! Are we not continuing to receive the fruit of these sacrifices?

Until the end of her life, her daily duties, the occupation and care of her home, her friendships and visits occupied Conchita's time and were the occasion to practice heroic virtues hidden in the midst of a most ordinary life. Attention to her sons and daughters-in-law, her son-in-law and the rest of her relatives, along with the help she could render to her grandchildren, continued until the end. She spent the last year of her life with her family in the house where she died, that of her son Ignatius, surrounded by her grandchildren.

The Lord wanted her life and her virtues to be completely susceptible to imitation, as were those of Mary, notwithstanding the extraordinary nature of the graces He had bestowed on His Servant.

Many years beforehand, the Lord had said to Conchita: *"You see, My daughter, as all of Mary's virtues were hidden, because of her humility, so also were her sorrows hidden. Accepting all of them, embracing all of them without losing any, adoring in them the Will of God, that was her life. The sorrows of absence."* The last months of the Servant of God were a faithful reflection of these words. Her children's testimony, "Mother always smiled," is profoundly significant. That smile was hiding a sea of suffering and bitterness, of which only her personal diary lets us have a glimpse.

The bitterness came of not knowing if Jesus loved her, nor if she loved Jesus. Bishop Martínez wrote to her on July 30, 1936, "It seems incredible that these two questions actually torture you: 'Does Jesus love me?' 'Do I love Him?'... Well, I assure you that God loves you very much. Betrothal; the Works of the Cross; Mystical Incarnation; renewal of Jesus' mysteries in your own life; spiritual maternity which has given you descendants like the stars of heaven and the sands of the sea; intimate confidences; the Internal Cross; your participation in Masses; the Third Love; ineffable participation in Jesus' sacrifice, sacrificing Him mystically; the consecration of your life to the glory of God and much, much more... and you still ask whether Jesus loves you?"

He tells her in this same letter, with good reason: "This is one of the most painful times of your life, but it is also one of the most fruitful."

With stunning simplicity, the last pages of her diary express what her life was and let us discern her immense pain and her desire, also immense, to always please the Lord: "I have remained in bed with much pain... offering everything up to my Jesus for His priests.

"Jesus, hidden... silent... asleep... and only His memory as a keepsake, an illusion that passed by, like a passion, a delirium that obscures everything and makes me cry. My God, have mercy on me! I have peace and delight in abandoning myself to the sweet and Most Holy Will of God.

"They had to rush a little grandchild to the hospital to operate on him....

"I am all alone and with so many daughters and with nobody to cure me. This is the way Jesus wants me to be and so, too, do I. May He be Blessed!"

And she finishes her diary, "Oh, my Jesus, may You be praised and everything be for Your glory!"

At another time, Jesus had told her, *"I desire to imprint My image in you, but sorrowfully...."* On her death-bed, the priest asked Conchita, "What about your relationship with Jesus?" She answered, "It is as if we had never known each other...."

Thirty-five years before, Conchita had written: "My God, my God, more than ever mine, because I am more than ever crucified and voluntarily crucified, have pity and mercy on me! If I have You, I will not experience having sorrow, even though my eyes do not see You, oh, Lord! Faith tells me that You are with those who suffer, with those who weep, embracing the cross. Do not allow me to let go of it, even if its heavy weight crushes me. I know that not everybody has the joy of dying as You, Lord: nailed to the cross and that only for the chosen is such a great happiness reserved. Although I do not deserve this grace, grant it to me through Your kindness, Lord. Today, Lord, on this anniversary of that grace, do not deny me this one which I ask of You with all my soul: to live upon the cross, to never come down from it and to die nailed to its arms; to pass from them into Your own arms, Lord, to bless You for all eternity."

The Lord responded to this prayer in the measure of her desire and her love and accomplished His promise: He imprinted His image upon Conchita... *"but sorrowfully."*

CONCLUSION

After having covered the spiritual journey of the Servant of God, Concepción Cabrera de Armida, at least in its great stages, considering them as a whole, some aspects of the divine calling stand out clearly, as well as the mission for which the Lord called her:

1. Even though her qualities and defects in her childhood and adolescence were like those of many others, the Divine Providence of God was already preparing her.

A yearning for God attracted her like a powerful magnet.

An infantile dream and her First Communion awakened in her soul a love for Jesus that kept on growing.

Her crucifix not only made her feel tenderness towards Him, but also propelled her to sacrifice herself joyfully for His love and to give Him souls.

The astonishing preservation of innocence and the purity of her soul refined her spiritual sensibility and prepared the cleanliness of her heart to "see" God and to transmit this message with fidelity.

Filial love for the Immaculate Virgin granted her a great love for purity, which would be one of her characteristics until the end of her days, as well as the desire to imitate Mary.

Beginning with the first stage, all these gifts of God point in one direction: the intimate union with Jesus crucified, on behalf of others, imitating Mary.

2. The Lord wanted her to marry *"for His lofty goals."* He wanted her to live the secular life, and as a spouse and widow she would attain the most profoundly transforming union with Jesus, not living for herself, but for others.

This was true from the first word she perceived within herself: *"Your mission is to save souls"*; the insistent words of her director: "Your mission is the cross"; the monogram upon her chest as a constant plea: "Jesus, Savior of mankind, save them"; the invitation of the Lord to drink from the chalice He would put to her lips; the presentation of the Cross of the Apostolate, symbol of her life and of her mission; the great suffering of body and soul; the graces of mystical union; the betrothal and the spiritual marriage. All of these graces took place during her married life and also pointed in one direction: the sanctity of secular and married life through intimate union with Jesus on the cross, in order to collaborate in the salvation of the world through loving sacrifice.

3. Her lived experience of the fruitfulness of marriage and motherly love prepared her for a spiritual motherhood — in imitation of Mary — of Jesus the Savior and of the thousands of spiritual children saved by Him and with Him in union with Mary, Mother of the Redeemer and Mother of the Church.

4. The central grace of her life, the Mystical Incarnation, and its immediate consequences: the full growth of her

baptismal priesthood; in the Chain of Love in offering up the Word; the words of the consecration, made her own, "This is My Body; this is My Blood," these gave her life and her mission a redemptive value and a sense of spiritual maternity which was profoundly priestly.

5. The last stage in union with and in imitation of Mary in her solitude, experiencing in her own soul the internal sorrows of Jesus's soul because of the sin that offends God and harms man, whom He loves, is a fruitful sacrifice for the Church. This fruitfulness makes itself somewhat perceptible in the enlightenment and promises regarding the kingdom of the Holy Spirit; in the priestly message, in the complete offering for the benefit of priests; and in the offering of her life and the lives of many others for the sanctification of homes. The Lord willed that the fruitfulness of Conchita's life and mission be directed toward two fundamental axes of the Church's life: priests and families.

6. Conchita's spiritual inheritance is not her own; it is of Jesus in her. The message of the Gospel is the message of the cross; it is Jesus's priestly oblation, the one He lived from His Incarnation until His death and shared with us; it is the reign of the Holy Spirit, the reign of holiness, to which the Lord invites us all; it is generous self-sacrifice on behalf of others.

The Works of the Cross, of which she is the spiritual mother — the works that must live the message of the cross — are God's works. She was the conduit and the instrument to carry them out.

7. The life, the message and the mission of the Servant of God contain a profound and divine unity by the Holy Spirit toward the intimate union with the Redeemer on behalf of mankind, with Mary and like Mary, Mother of Jesus and of the Church, for the glory of the Father. *"I want to imprint on you My own image... but a painful image...."* *"You were born for others... you do not belong to yourself."*

APPENDIX

R eading these pages, you have frequently encountered the expression: "The Lord said to Conchita." You have undoubtedly asked yourselves if these words are heard with one's ears, or in the imagination, or in what manner this occurs. According to scholars of mystical theology, the answer is that this almost always relates to intellectual visions, which are less likely to lend themselves to illusion or error. But instead of explaining it with my own words, I prefer to transcribe some pages in which the Servant of God tries to explain it, and others, in which it is the Lord Who makes her see it.

"Sometimes I do not want to listen and I listen; I do not want to understand and I understand; I do not want to turn around, I may say, toward the Lord, so as not to see myself engaged and He comes to meet me; He reproaches me and He compels me.

"Sometimes He dictates to me, more or less, with phrases or words; other times not so, but all at once He imprints a stream of things inside of me, sometimes very briefly, but leaving in me a clear intelligence of what has come through, of what is to come... sometimes little by little, and other times, all of a sudden. My senses quiet themselves as a signal that the Lord is coming and so do my faculties, leaving me as a white paper, as though emptied of myself and of every worldly noise. Thus, without coordinating ideas, I receive an inference of interior words, or already ordered concepts; let us say that I understand all of a sudden.

"I interrupt these thoughts or interior talks with questions, with feelings, and this is transformed into a conversation, into dialogues that the Lord deigns to satisfy by explaining them to me. When I reflect, I have already questioned Him; I have interrupted Him with my lack of manners, but by the time I am conscious of what I have done, I have already done it.

"I do not hear a voice with my corporal ears, except perhaps a few times. Sometimes I am tempted to believe that I am inventing it all, that I am deceived, but when I am at peace, I cannot doubt that these things come from God.

"Besides that, in my experience, when the Lord does not give, I may spend hours in prayer, yet I cannot even write a line by myself; I am without juice, all dried up, without being able to invent, even if I desired to do so. I suffer when I imagine that I deceive myself and I would prefer not to be given credit, for I believe I would be more at ease. Then I remember that one time, I was very distressed with Father Alzola about fooling myself and it made me laugh when he answered, 'Let us suppose that you wish to deceive. Do you believe we would be so foolish as to believe it?' With this the temptation went away.

"Sometimes months go by and the Lord does not speak to me, and others, I hardly have time to write all He says to me. Another way in which the Lord communicates with me has been by writing. Many times when I am praying or at another time, I have heard His voice say to me, *'Write.'* At the beginning, I resisted and instantly I was filled with dryness — such aridity — until I began to obey; at the very moment of taking up the pencil, the Lord started to spill Himself out, dictating sheets and sheets, sometimes about lofty theological items, they say, which I never could have invented myself.

"'*Your writing is prayer,*' the Lord has told me when I felt remorse about setting myself to write and He recommended only that I accomplish my duties first, striving after that to glorify Him in this way."

On another page, the Lord Himself explained to her:

"*Also, the manner of communicating Myself to you involves the aspect of unity because, in God, everything is one. For example, I reflect Myself in the mirror or crystal of your soul. Those divine rays remain there and you, experiencing yourself touched by them, start to see, to contemplate and to understand.*

"*And afterwards, with the help of your mind, you give them form with the words that you more or less suitably adapt, that of which I Myself, without your realizing it, have left the substance. In the first streak of light you trace the essence, the photograph of the communicated thing in your soul, to your intellectual faculties, and from there to the paper.*

"*In this manner of communication of God with the creature there is almost never a mistake, except if human passions come to involve themselves; then they obscure and twist and even erase the signs of God in the soul.*

"*This is a mode of communication from God, derived from His unity, when with one blow He imprints that which the creature takes afterward and gives to it an earthly language, although even for this, divine cooperation is necessary.*

"When a soul receives this communication humbly and lends itself to it with purity of heart, which is essential, without mixing in any passion, God's impression is clear, clean and luminous, and there is no danger of mistake.

"Surely, when the divine comes through the human, it takes the form or color of the receptacle receiving these communications, but this is secondary. The essence, the substance and even the form remains the same that God was willing to communicate.

"My daughter, thus because of My goodness and for My high goals, I have made of you an instrument or an aqueduct. Never stain the mirror of your soul, because now I need you more than ever clean, clear and transparent, to communicate the outpouring of the Holy Spirit's graces. Do not lift up your glance and do not ever be proud; lower it always. Look for Me in the hidden mirror of your soul, and you will find Me there, and there will you listen to Me, and there you will understand the marvels of your only and unique God, that has His delight in making Himself known to humble souls, for the good of many souls that will give Him glory."

I want to name the bishops and priests who, in one way or another, had a providential intervention in the spiritual journey of the Servant of God. Those who had a more profound relationship with her and helped her more effectively in her spiritual life and in her works and those who, at the same time, fell under her influence, which was in many cases decisive, towards sanctity.

a. The bishops who dealt with her most closely and who supported her from the first moment: Bishop Leopoldo Ruíz y Flores (Archbishop and future Apostolic Delegate), Bishop Ramón Ibarra y González (Archbishop of Puebla), Bishop Luís M. Martínez (Primate Archbishop of México), Bishop Miguel de la Mora (Archbishop of San Luís Potosí) and Father Félix de Jesús Rougier, founder and Superior General of the Missionaries of the Holy Spirit.

b. Priests who were her spiritual directors, confessors, or counselors and were afterwards bishops and continued to support the Servant of God: Father Maximino Ruíz (Bishop of Chiapas), Father Emeterio Valverde y Téllez (Bishop of León), Father Enrique Sánchez Paredes (Archbishop of Puebla), Father Laureano Veres (Bishop of New York), Father Guillermo Tritschler y Córdoba (Archbishop of Monterrey), Father Pascual Díaz (Archbishop of México) and Father Ignacio Márquez (Archbishop of Puebla).

c. The Provincial Fathers: Alzola and Ipiña (Jesuits), Cepeda (Claretian).

d. The learned and virtuous priests and religious: Carrera, Mayer, Dauvergne, Soler (Jesuits), Cedeño (from the Oratory), Daydí (Paulist), Buitrón (canon), Jose Guadalupe Treviño, M.Sp.S.

e. The ones who were disinterested or contrary at first and afterwards profoundly appreciated the spirit and the heroic virtue of the Servant of God: Bishops Sbarretti (Cardinal), Alarcón (Archbishop of México), Mora y del Río (Archbishop of México), Plancarte and Navarrete (Archbishops of Monterrey).

Many others interacted with her more distantly, but appreciated her spirit and virtues, such as Bishop Ortíz (Guadalajara), Herrera and Piña (Monterrey), Echeverría (Saltillo), Vanegas (Querétaro).

BIBLIOGRAPHY

All of the sources of this work are unpublished works of the Venerable Concepción Cabrera de Armida.

General

Autobiography - first and second part; one volume.
Life [*Vida*] - nine volumes.
Spiritual Diary [*Cuenta de Conciencia*] - sixty-six volumes.

Specific

First Stage: *Autobiography, Life* [*Vida*], and *Diary,* Volumes 1 and 45.

Second Stage: *Autobiography, Life,* and *Diary,* Volumes 1, 3, 8, 9, 13, 14, 17.

Third Stage: *Diary,* Volumes 18, 22, 23, 24, 38-41.

Fourth Stage: *Diary,* Volumes 41, 42, 43, 45-66.